T0319840

Islamic Education in the United States and the Evolution of Muslim Nonprofit Institutions

NEW HORIZONS IN NONPROFIT RESEARCH

Series Editors: Bruce A. Seaman *and* Dennis R. Young, *Andrew Young School of Policy Studies, Georgia State University, USA*

The purpose of this series is to publish monographs and edited collections of original research that address previously understudied aspects of the social economy and civil society worldwide. The series will include theoretical and empirical research, with an emphasis on nonprofit organizations and social enterprises, including their internal management, governance and leadership challenges, and the changing economic, social, political and public policy environments in which they operate. The series will be interdisciplinary in character, with a particular emphasis on economics, management science and public policy analysis, but also embracing works based in other social science disciplines, including political science, sociology, psychology and anthropology. The series will also take a broad view of the social economy, to include the many service fields and industries in which nonprofit organizations, social purpose cooperatives, social purpose businesses, public–private partnerships and other forms of social purpose enterprise operate. Preference will be given to research with practical implications for management, governance and public policy, and to works which define new agendas for future research.

Islamic Education in the United States and the Evolution of Muslim Nonprofit Institutions

Sabith Khan

Assistant Professor, California Lutheran University, USA

Shariq Siddiqui

Executive Director, Association for Research on Nonprofit Organizations and Voluntary Action, USA; Visiting Assistant Professor and Director, Muslim Philanthropy Initiative, Lilly Family School of Philanthropy, Indiana University, USA

NEW HORIZONS IN NONPROFIT RESEARCH

Cheltenham, UK • Northampton, MA, USA

Published by
Edward Elgar Publishing Limited
The Lypiatts
15 Lansdown Road
Cheltenham
Glos GL50 2JA
UK

Edward Elgar Publishing, Inc.
William Pratt House
9 Dewey Court
Northampton
Massachusetts 01060
USA

A catalogue record for this book
is available from the British Library

Library of Congress Control Number: 2017947236

This book is available electronically in the **Elgar**online
Social and Political Science subject collection
DOI 10.4337/9781786434807

ISBN 978 1 78643 479 1 (cased)
ISBN 978 1 78643 480 7 (eBook)

Typeset by Servis Filmsetting Ltd, Stockport, Cheshire
Printed and bound by CPI Group (UK) Ltd, Croydon, CR0 4YY

Dedicated to:

My parents: Fazlulla Khan and Samiunnisa. Two life-long public school teachers, who taught me everything about giving of one's self and resources; My teachers: In particular, Professor Joyce Rothschild who helped me become a better scholar; My wife: Fabiola Lara, who taught me the meaning of patience and persistence.

– Sabith Khan

My parents: Sumera and Nasim Siddiqui who taught me the value of philanthropy and a life of service; My children: Fatima, Amal, Safaa and Zaki who have shown me the beauty of philanthropy; My wife: Sobia Khan who is my rock, my harbor, my day and night. With her by my side – all is possible.

– Shariq Siddiqui

To the staff and volunteers of Islamic schools: who sacrifice so much so children can retain their religious and cultural identity while maintaining exceptional academics.

Contents

Figures

Foreword
Evolution of religious nonprofits in the US: a brief history
David C. Hammack

Sabith Khan and Shariq Siddiqui make an excellent point when they insist at the outset of this very useful study that Islamic schools, houses of worship, and charities in the United States have found the laws and practices of the nation's religious nonprofit sector "indispensable." This foreword undertakes to suggest why American laws are so important.

As Khan and Siddiqui emphasize, under the laws, regulations, practices, and understandings that govern American nonprofit organizations, American Muslim institutions operate autonomously and voluntarily, guided by their own boards, setting their own missions, following their own rules. Like other American nonprofits, they can own property, make contracts, hire and fire employees, provide and charge fees for educational and other services. They are usually exempt from state and local property and sales taxes; their donors can generally subtract gifts from the personal income subject to federal as well as state tax. To religious entities of any sort, these are critically valuable rights and privileges.

These powerful advantages under the American nonprofit regime do come with limitations. To exercise their rights and privileges, schools and other operating charities must organize in a formal way. The American processes for incorporation under state law and for seeking federal as well as state and local tax exemption are not onerous, but they must be followed. More significantly, American nonprofits must refrain from distributing surplus income as profits, and must persuade people to support them with time, expertise and money. To maintain full religious autonomy, they must decide not to seek direct government subsidies.

Religious nonprofit organizations must follow fundamental laws, especially laws relating to health and safety within their facilities; they must observe the laws respecting criminal behavior; they must honor contracts and pay their debts. To retain maximum autonomy, all nonprofits must eschew government funding and rely only on donations and earned income. And they must observe basic rules – including special federal rules relating to international fundraising and international giving – as they appeal for funds, charge for tuition and other services, and make gifts or provide services overseas.

Religious communities can find that American law complicates efforts to establish and maintain orthodoxy. Individuals, and members of communities acting as individuals, can decide to support particular interpretations of religious ideas and practice, and to apply social sanctions to those who disagree. But it is very difficult to use American law, or the powers of American governments, to force others to accept and abide by any particular interpretation of religious obligation.

These American laws and practices regarding religious organizations have deep historical roots. Revolutionary-era writings made occasional reference to Jews and Muslims, but Christian conflicts between Protestants and Catholics, and especially conflicts among Protestant sects, constituted the context for early developments in the US. The conflicts among Protestants are too often neglected, but they were decisive. Britain had made sometimes strenuous efforts to use its established national church to help rule its American colonies, in ways that increasingly infuriated the colonists. Britain's practices derived in part from the Protestant split from the Catholic Church, but they reflected conflict among Protestants as well. (British policy could also reflect "reason of state" as when, after the conquest of Quebec, it recognized the Catholic Church in the territory along the St. Lawrence River seized from France to the consternation of many colonial Protestants.) Through the Church of England, English leaders had worked to tamp down Puritan demands for rigorous uniformity (in Old England as well as in New England), to limit the influence of Presbyterians, Mennonites, Lutherans, Baptists in the colonies as well as at home, to displace the Dutch Reformed in the American colonies, and on both sides of the Atlantic to limit, marginalize or silence Quakers, and Unitarians. Church of England leaders had mostly sided with the home country during the Revolutionary War. After the war, the other denominations sought revenge against the Episcopalian heirs of the English Church – and fought one another for material advantage, and to enact laws consistent with their religious preferences.

All this provided the impetus for the adoption of the religion clauses of the First Amendment to the US Constitution:

> Congress shall make no law respecting an establishment of religion, or prohibiting the free exercise thereof.

America's nonprofit laws put these clauses, together with the other clauses of the First Amendment or abridging the freedom of speech, or of the press; or the right of the people peaceably to assemble, and to petition the Government for a redress of grievances

into effect. The protections of religious rights are especially strict: for most of the twentieth century Congress has interpreted them to preclude census-takers from asking individuals or organizations to provide information about their organizations – including about their finances.

Britain had almost always forbidden the public practice of Catholicism in its American colonies, and for a century or more after Independence many American Protestants did what they could to discourage the development of Catholic institutions. But despite strong opposition both to some Catholic beliefs and to the international and hierarchical character of Catholic leadership, American courts generally allowed Catholics to build, maintain, and defend churches and schools, and soon charities as well. Some states made it difficult for Catholics to use their international institutions to control churches and clergy in the United States, but by the twentieth century, the Catholic right to exercise those powers was well established. Leaders of business, of civic organizations, and of political parties could seek the good will of Catholics, or of members of other religious communities, by providing material, political, and moral support to relevant organizations, and by directing aid to members of a community that had suffered from disaster, in the United States or abroad, through its religious organizations.

Before the Great Society's addition of health care and anti-discrimination responsibilities to the federal government, state laws greatly surpassed federal laws in their religious impact. Voters paid attention to the laws and regulations relating to their religious communities, and as the numbers of Catholic (or Jewish, or Lutheran, or Baptist . . .) voters increased, laws and their enforcement changed to accommodate the growing group. In the give and take of American politics, this often meant that a group whose numbers were rising did not have to become one of the largest in a city or a state before others accepted its religious claims or agreed that its members should be protected from discrimination and abuse. By the same token, groups that found themselves excluded from the electorate also found their religious institutions scorned and left at a disadvantage. African Americans suffered most obviously in this way, but the same was true of Native Americans, Mexican Americans, and immigrants who had not yet become citizens. As Muslims, like Hindus and followers of other world religions, have become more and more numerous and prominent in parts of the United States, they have created their own organizations to take their places in the nation's religious nonprofit sector.

In this book, Sabith Khan and Shariq Siddiqui show how America's Muslim communities are recognizing and making use of the possibilities afforded by nonprofit status in the United States. The experience of other religious communities suggests that Muslim nonprofits will find significant opportunities to build religious, educational, and other institutions to sustain beliefs into the next generation, to engage with fellow believers, to demonstrate beliefs through service and active engagement with others, and to advocate for recognition. If the experiences of others suggest a guide, the challenges will include maintaining engagement with and support from fellow believers, negotiating the laws relating to international as well as domestic fundraising, developing alliances with non-Muslim religious nonprofits, and negotiating the changing environment for government funding.

In the United States, religious institutions have always sought government funding for their charitable work, including their work in education and health care. In the nineteenth century this often led to a settlement under which municipal or state governments underwrote much of the costs of orphanages, while conferring on schools, clinics, and burial grounds only tax-exemption advantages. Great Society programs made federal money available for healthcare covered by Medicare and Medicaid; subsequent federal programs expanded funding for some kinds of job training and some support for children with development or socialization challenges. In the last two decades, the school choice movement and shifting court decisions on the "separation of church and state" have brought some increase in the availability of tax funds for elementary and secondary education – but the total proportion of children in nonpublic schools has not increased, and in some places has declined. Money always has a price: religious groups that seek government funds must accept government rules. In turn, each group that obtains government funds has an incentive to ally with others who seek changes to the rules.

As Khan and Sidiqqui make clear, American Muslim communities are finding a substantial role for religious nonprofits as they address their pressing concerns. There is much to explore. With this book, the exploration is well begun.

David C. Hammack is Hiram C. Haydn Professor of History at Case Western Reserve University, USA. David has written extensively on the history of America's civil society, nonprofit organizations, and philanthropic foundations, and on the history of cities, the built environment, and education.

Preface

During the last twenty years, the study of charity and philanthropy has grown enormously. Empirical approaches to the study of generosity have shaped our understanding of both the quantity and the motivations of giving. In addition to this rise in the study of "Voluntary Action" there has been an explosion of academic courses in Nonprofit Management. With philanthropic giving at historic levels, exceeding $350 billion, we are also witnessing a rapid rise in interest in the study of the phenomenon of giving, more generally.

Within this context, our book *Islamic Education in the United States and the Evolution of Muslim Nonprofit Institutions* offers an in-depth look at a small subset of this vibrant philanthropic landscape in the US: Muslim American communities. This subsector has suffered from three key problems: First, there has been a lack of academic study using empirical methods. Second, there has been a tendency to look at aspects of Islamic philanthropy purely from a national security perspective. From this perspective, philanthropy is seen as either supporting global militant movements or countering them. There is no nuanced perspective on why Muslim Americans give locally or globally, their motivations for doing so and the causes that they support. Third, Muslim American nonprofits are being held accountable not for mistakes that they have made but because of a generalized public perception of potential abuse by the sector. Our approach has been to move away from these existing lacunae and look at this phenomenon of giving from a sociological lens – to critically examine how and why Muslim Americans give to schools.

Given the controversial nature of how the discourse of Islamic schools has been shaped in the US, we believe this impartial examination of philanthropy, using empirical methods, will aid in clarifying some of the misconceptions and stereotypes about these schools and will also demystify the role of philanthropy as well as public funding for them.

We address questions on the scope of private philanthropy, the role of public funding – whether it is through grants or voucher programs – and also other forms of government support. In addition, through extensive interviews with board members and principals of these schools, we delve into how these schools manage their "Islamic" identity and what makes them distinct, if at all.

Despite having worked in the sector for some time, we were surprised by some of the findings. We hope this book contributes to the scholarship on Muslim American institutions and philanthropic giving, offering an objective assessment of perhaps the most diverse religious group in the US.

Acknowledgments

This book began as a research paper authored by the two of us. What started as a simple idea from Shariq turned out to be a well-received conference paper at the Association for Research on Nonprofit and Voluntary Action (ARNOVA). This led to other ideas and papers, and eventually blossomed into a proposal for a book. This project has as much to do with serendipity as it has with patience and persistence.

We met at the Lilly School of Philanthropy in 2013, during Sabith's research stint at the Center on Philanthropy. We have both benefited from the scholarly community at the Indiana University–Purdue University Indianapolis (IUPUI), which could be considered our "intellectual home" of sorts. All the wonderful scholars and practitioners there have provided us with the inspiration, guidance and support to enable us to be scholars of philanthropy. We have benefited from this association immensely.

The scholarly community at ARNOVA is another big source of guidance, support and inspiration. This core group of scholars has shaped, and continues to shape, the discourse of voluntary action and giving in the US and around the world. As one of the most intellectually engaged communities, we have both learned a lot and remain grateful for our friendships with scholars at ARNOVA.

Finally, the friendships that we have formed during our doctoral education are worthy of mention. In no particular order, Khaldoun AbouAssi, Una Osili, Peter Frumkin, David King, Daisha Merritt, Arjen De Wit, Greg Witkowksi, Lehn Benjamin, Dwight Burlingame, David Craig, Safaa Zarzour, Basharat Saleem, Mukhtar Ahmad, Joyce Rothschild, Marc Stern, Yang Zhang, Reza Aslan, Paul Schervish, the Islamic Society of North America, the Council of Islamic Schools in North America, the Sister Clara Muhammad Schools Foundation and the Islamic School League of North America have been extremely generous with their time and feedback.

Our editor, Alan Sturmer, deserves a particular debt of gratitude for his patience and guidance as we worked through the various stages of this book – from a proposal to the first draft and then the final version. Finally, we are grateful to the editors of the series, Dennis Young and Bruce Seaman, for their willingness to further our field by shining the spotlight on an understudied area of philanthropic studies.

Sponsors

This book was made possible through the generous financial support of:

Hamzavi Family Foundation
Ismail & Uzma Mehr
Khalique Zahir
Center on Muslim Philanthropy
Association of Muslim Nonprofit Professionals
Dr Ibad Ansari and Family

1. Introduction

The election of 2016 may prove to be a turning point in Muslim American participation in the public sphere and also for institution building among the Muslim American communities. While the election campaign that brought Donald J. Trump to power was marked by extreme levels of xenophobia and Islamophobia, that trend has not died down with him in power as the President of the United States. Although there are indications that Muslim communities are coming together with each other, and with other faith-based groups and secular ones as well, the challenges of addressing xenophobia are still big. In the realm of education and particularly faith-based education, the discourse of Islam plays out in ways that are not always positive. However, looking at the landscape of Islamic education in the US, one cannot miss the dynamism and dedication of those who work in the sector.

Islamic education in the US is coming into its own. As the number of mosques (also called Islamic centers) in the US continues to grow, there is a concomitant rise in the number of Islamic schools that offer K-12 level education. Although previous studies such as *Educating the Muslims of America* by Yvonne Haddad, Farid Senzai and Jane Smith (Haddad et al., 2009) have shown us the various dimensions of curricula and the cultural landscape of these schools, much remains to be said. At the same time, there is also a growing suspicion of these schools, which is an indication of the prevalent xenophobia in our society. Haddad et al. argue for the role of Islamic schools to be one of centers of culture preservation and transfer of knowledge – both traditional and modern. This is the starting point of our thesis; we then build on this insight to offer a perspective on how the role of Islamic schools has evolved over the decades.

An article in *The Atlantic* gives voice to these concerns.[1] The fear of "indoctrination" of children in public schools is supposed to be one of the concerns among many who are opposed to the presence of curricula or assignments that deal with Islam. Related to that is the fear of Islamic schools and Muslim communities in the US. This fear has become real, especially since 9/11, and it has manifested in many ugly ways, from protests by parents to school boards to demonstrations in front of mosques and other religious institutions, as *The Atlantic* article points out. While the fear complex generated about Islamic schools is real, so is their presence. The Islamic schools are in the business of preserving religious knowledge, traditions and culture, in a safe environment.

While the political atmosphere may not be entirely conducive for those who are involved in teaching Islam, there seems to be a growing interest in the teaching of Islam in the realms of higher education. The events of 9/11 marked a watershed moment for this, with enrollment of students reaching record levels, especially for those wanting to study Islam or the Middle East.

The Muslim American civil society seems vibrant too, with a growing number of Islamic centers, Sunday schools and informal learning groups, or *halaqas*, that come together to learn and teach about Islam. There are also full-time K-12 schools – the very focus of this book – in addition to *Hifz* schools, where children are taught the nuances of the Qur'an through interpretation and also learn to memorize it. As Haddad et al. point out, the appeal of Islamic schools arises for various reasons: they help preserve and promote Islamic values, they protect children from the bullying and taunting that can occur in public schools, and they also protect the children from the effects of drugs and alcohol, as well as from premarital sex.

On the other hand, the debate about school vouchers, government support of private schools, is also impacting this sector. While most of the schools cater to middle-class, suburban and educated Muslims and a few non-Muslims, the factors impinging on these schools are the same as those that affect other faith-based schools. The question of religion in the public sphere in the US is a tricky one, and if that religion happens to be Islam, then, given the particular challenges that Muslim communities are facing, this question becomes even more acute.

This book attempts to contextualize the Muslim American nonprofit sector, in addition to offering a detailed view of the Islamic schools' landscape. We aim to achieve this through a historical analysis of the factors that were responsible for the success of Muslim American institution building and also for their propagation. We contend that the earlier waves of Muslim migration to America did not result in the preservation of Muslim cultures or Islamic traditions, and it is only more recently that Muslims have been able to preserve and propagate their Islamic values and norms. While the earliest expressions of Islam in the US, through the founding of the Nation of Islam (NOI), were particularistic and unique to the US, these expressions have often existed in tandem and at times in opposition to global discourses of orthodox Islam. The history of Islamic education in the US is as complex as the history of Islam there. Our attempt involves unpacking this history through looking at the evolution of Islamic schools and the leadership challenges, the policy environment and the philanthropic contributions that were made towards them.

The nonprofit model, as it exists, has been indispensable for this process. As Siddiqui points out, "ISNA's quest for legitimacy was aided by its adherence to its core value of being an American religious nonprofit organization rather than an international Islamic movement. This embrace of volunteeristic, pluralistic, and democratic values helped the organization sustain its identity and develop internal and external legitimacy" (2014, p. 3). If one sees the Islamic Society of North America (ISNA) as a paradigmatic case of a Muslim American nonprofit, one can see how it has evolved as an American institution with its own unique Islamic identity. This story is being repeated throughout the country, with small variations. As Muqtedar Khan, a scholar of Islam in America, points out, earlier Muslims were fighting to preserve their Muslimness, but now they are fighting to preserve their Americanness (Khan, 2002). The Muslim American nonprofit sector, and in particular the Islamic education space, allows us to understand the evolution of Muslim American practices in the American context.

Further, we contend that the process of evolution of Muslim American institutions has occurred despite the various constraints that were placed on the communities – initially legal, as immigration was restricted from Asia until the opening of doors in 1965 with the Hart–Cellar Act. More recent developments have helped, and in some cases forced, the Muslim American communities to be active participants in American civil society.

GLOBAL DISCOURSES, LOCAL CHALLENGES: THE GROWTH AND EVOLUTION OF MUSLIM AMERICAN NONPROFITS[2]

The literature around Islam in America, Muslim civil society and philanthropy is vast. This covers the gamut of diaspora studies, American studies, philanthropic studies and Middle Eastern studies. The seminal works in this area are focused on showing how Islam is compatible with American values. In doing so, they examine Muslims in America as external entities. These studies seek to examine how Muslim Americans fare in America, rather than how they actually participate in America (GhaneaBassiri, 2010, p. 4). The focus of these studies is to see how Muslim Americans are able to mediate "foreign" values within an American context. They either look at the ability of Muslim Americans to take distinct Islamic values and translate them into a distinct American practice or they examine whether

American society is open to these values. These studies focus on convincing their audience that Islam is compatible with American society.

The second set of important works focuses on specific ethnic groups of Muslims in America (Curtis, 2006; Leonard, 1997, 2007; Abraham and Shyrock, 2000; Naff, 1985; Elkholy, 1966). With the exception of Edward Curtis, each of these describes each ethnic group as though they stand in isolation in American society. Curtis examines how Black Muslims in the NOI sought to define themselves not only by how they saw themselves within their movement but also in conjunction with the larger Muslim community.

The third set of scholarship includes collections of works of Muslim Americans' essays that aid in illustrating a range of issues related to Muslims in America. These collections are invaluable for the study of Islam in America, yet do not provide a comprehensive analysis or connect the dots for the reader (Haddad, 2002; Haddad and Esposito, 1998; Haddad and Smith, 1994; Curtis, 2008, 2010).[3] Furthermore, this self-articulation by Muslim Americans, while vital, does not provide a global historical context.

These major works tend to examine Muslim Americans within the context of separate ethnic groups: African Americans and immigrants. Those seeking to expand upon these groups see Islam in America through singular lenses of African Americans, Arabs, Asians and others.

We suggest that looking at the case of ISNA, as a paradigmatic case study, can tell us a lot about the dynamics within the Muslim American non-governmental organization (NGO) sector.

ISNA has also been the focus of four important scholars. Steve Johnson examines ISNA in Yvonne Haddad and Jane Smith's important book *Muslim Communities in North America* (Johnson, 1994). Johnson's work is based on available research and personal interviews of Muslims in Indianapolis prior to 1994. His work looks at ISNA from its inception to 1990. He finds that in 1990 "Islam at an institutional level in Indianapolis is in flux." (Johnson, 1994). His study shows that during the period around the First Gulf War the alliances and relationships had changed in nature, and the work also confirms our assertion that the initial founders of ISNA included Historically Sunni African American Muslims (HSAAMs) such as Dr. Ihsan Bagby and Umar Khattab.

He also confirms the division between HSAAMs and African American Muslims such as the community of Imam Warith Deen Muhammad. In addition, his chapter shows the constant struggles among activist, indigenous and cultural pluralist Muslim Americans. However, in his chapter he fails to comprehend the divisions between the two immigrant groups that were a part of ISNA. He understands the divisions to be either ethnic or religious and argues that the divisions are generally along

"conservative-liberal, socioeconomic, and immigrant-indigenous lines."
We show that divisions exist among immigrants and within the indigenous
Muslim American communities that cannot be placed simply within a
socioeconomic or conservative-liberal framework. Muslim Americans who
were similarly situated economically, religiously and ethnically had different visions for Islam in America. Steve Johnson's chapter is important
in confirming the tensions between the groups that existed, but it fails to
explain the nature of the disagreement.

Gutbi Mahdi Ahmed attempts to study Muslim organizations in the
US around the same period as Johnson (Ahmed, 1991). Ahmed helps
confirm the initial development of ISNA as a continuation of the work by
the Federation of Islamic Associations of the United States and Canada
(FIA) and the Muslim Student Association of the US & Canada (MSA).
He also shows how ISNA adopted the conference and publication format
of the FIA. However, he fails to understand the important role that the
FIA has played in the development of ISNA. He also fails to demonstrate
that ISNA, like the FIA, was meeting the needs of its constituent Muslim
Americans at the time. The FIA was formed by Muslim American World
War II veterans who were focusing on the needs of a population that
was largely born in the US. ISNA was formed after the massive influx of
immigrants from all over the Muslim world. He confirms Siddiqui's dissertation's assertion that in the early part of ISNA's history, its conventions
generally featured international Muslim speakers.

Ahmed sees ISNA as a branch of the larger transnational, international
and diasporic Muslim movements, such as the Muslim Brotherhood. He
fails to understand that these internationalist activists represent only one
of the founding groups of ISNA. He argues that ISNA is considered to
be "the national Muslim organization and generally represents the Islamic
mainstream." However, he fails to define "mainstream," and by virtue
of his description of ISNA, he assumes that it excludes indigenous, non-
activist and American-born Muslims. His chapter also fails to illustrate
the rich interaction between ISNA and Imam Warith Deen Muhammad
and other groups that existed in the US. While his work provides a good
overview of the organization, it does not probe the deeper interactions
of its founders, the role of American history in ISNA's development, or
how ISNA is placed within the development of Muslim American institution building. He views ISNA as an organization that came to America,
reformed Islamic work, embedded it in a "firm ideological structure" and
then incorporated enough American-born Muslims to become a national
organization. This analysis fails to show that, in fact, ISNA was the result
of Muslim American participation in institution building that was shaped
by the changing landscape in the US and American religious history.

Karen Leonard helps us understand the important role of ISNA within the broader context of Muslim American institution building (Leonard, 2003). Leonard also outlines the important role that the changing Muslim American population played in the establishment of ISNA. However, her analysis of ISNA supposes that a largely Arabic-speaking immigrant community established ISNA. The role of HSAAMs and non-Arabs in ISNA is missing from her analysis. Leonard also marks important changes in ISNA's positions but does not identify the tensions and transitions between the three founding groups within ISNA as a source of these changes.

Leonard tends to examine Muslim Americans within the context of separate ethnic groups: African Americans and immigrants. She further separates immigrants based on their national or regional identities. Leonard specifically argues that in this post-1990 environment, South Asians had control of major Muslim American organizations (2003, p. 12). In this analysis, we seek to show that, although this may seem true on the surface, an analysis based on ethnic or national identity does injustice to the deeper ideological tensions within those groups. Some of the ideological tensions were common across those national and ethnic identities. South Asians had become major funders of ISNA but still continued to elect a diverse group of Muslim American leaders who reflected the South Asians' ideology, not their ethnic identity. Had ethnic identity been the most important aspect in the calculus of these South Asian Muslims, the Islamic Circle of North America (ICNA) would have served as a better host as it was primarily established to serve the Indian and Pakistani Muslim American identity. However, what we will see is that, although ISNA thrived on diversity, ICNA and MAS (Muslim American Society, an Arab organization) were on a course of either decline or stagnant growth until they adopted similar approaches to diversity. However, Leonard's analysis provides us with insight on how different the leadership of Muslim American organizations appeared.

Finally, GhaneaBassiri provides us with the most important framework of Muslim American history within which to place ISNA. Kambiz GhaneaBassiri's work helps us move away from the historical perception of Islam as foreign to America. He argues that Muslim American history should be seen as a relational history of a distinct people of faith over a period of time (GhaneaBassiri, 2010). GhaneaBassiri suggests that rather than studying Muslim Americans as being distinct from America and its history, they should be studied through their participation in American society. Muslim Americans stand at the intersection of American religious history and modern Islamic history.

GhaneaBassiri provides us with the most comprehensive analysis of the history of Islam in America. His book shows how Muslim Americans have "defined themselves in relation to the changing conceptions of race, religious pluralism, and national identity in the United States." GhaneaBassiri helps us place ISNA within the larger history of Muslim American institution building, specifically its relationship with grassroots institution building and institutions. He argues, as we do, that American history played an important role in shaping Muslim-American institution building. He also shows the diversity of Muslim American institutions such as ICNA, the NOI, and Imam Warith Deen Muhammad's community that operated successfully at the same time as ISNA.

Finally, he demonstrates that they all sought to reach out to a much broader audience than those who founded the organization. They had similar delivery methods: They all held conventions, published magazines and provided speakers and materials to the grassroots organizations. They all delivered their programs and materials in English to reach out to a diverse Muslim American population. However, they did not act in a vacuum, and there was a great deal of interaction between these national organizations and ISNA.

His analysis also explores the debate within ISNA over the role of Muslim Americans in society. ISNA's decision to urge Muslim Americans to become involved in politics created controversy. The debate within ISNA mirrored the debate within Muslim Americans at large. His work shows the establishment of important organizations such as the Muslim Public Affairs Council (MPAC), the Council on American–Islamic Relations (CAIR) and the Muslim American Society (MAS). However, his analysis does not show the reason why former leaders of ISNA established these organizations instead of implementing those programs within ISNA. Furthermore, his analysis fails to show that the interaction between these groups may have helped change minds. People who were former activists later joined the progressives, and vice versa. Muslim American ideological positions did not remain static and did not move in a singular direction.

MUSLIM AMERICAN PHILANTHROPY: WHAT DO WE KNOW?

The bulk of Muslim American philanthropy can be understood through studies on Muslim institution building in the US (Haddad and Smith, 1994). Therefore, what is lacking is an analysis of this institution building and Muslim American philanthropy within the context of faith and giving. Also missing is an analysis of Muslim American civic engagement within the context of philanthropic studies.

In 1981, at the time of ISNA's inception, the nonprofit sector in the

US was fertile ground for the establishment of a new Muslim American organization. Walter Powell and Richard Steinberg's (2006) collection outlines the historical, religious, political, social and cultural influences that went into developing this sector. Peter Hall's overview of the history of the nonprofit and voluntary sector in the US helps us overlay the Muslim engagement in this sector (Hall, 2006). Muslim American civic engagement in general mirrors the trends among nonprofits in America during the same period.

Economic theories like the "three-failures theory" have long been used to justify the existence of a nonprofit sector (Powell and Steinberg, 2006). However, as Richard Steinberg (2006) admits, these economic theories are incomplete. Economic theories articulate why consumers want to donate to nonprofits but fail to explain why nonprofits exist in the first place. In fact, organizations like ISNA were not established just to offer missing services; they also sought to shape the way Muslim Americans and non-Muslims think about Islam and Muslims. This perspective is missing from the economic theories, but Steinberg helps to integrate some of these questions in his chapter. ISNA fits within the framework of nonprofit theory within the US and can be understood using the same lens that we use to study other American nonprofits. Far too often, scholars make the mistake of focusing on the increasingly foreign-looking nature of the organization's membership and leadership and then seek answers through a foreign lens.

However, as Cadge and Wuthnow (2006) point out, it would be a mistake to look at ISNA from the general prism of a nonprofit organization. The role of religion is not understood as well in earlier philanthropic studies, despite the strong role it has played in American civic life. "Long before social scientists and policy makers identified 'nonprofits' as composing a distinct social sector, religion offered ways of carrying out social activities that differed from those of either the marketplace or government," they contend. ISNA understood the important role that grassroots Muslim organizations played in the congregational, spiritual and social lives of Muslim Americans and sought to harness that important resource by using the tools that the nonprofit sector used. ISNA, like many religious organizations, had to find a way to balance the special role of the nonprofit sector with its religious practices. Not all decisions that a religious nonprofit organization makes are based on nonprofit best practices. Organizations like ISNA rely on their religious values, which at times are in tension with the current political landscape.

ISNA established itself as a membership-based organization. This choice has traditionally been attributed to the fact that many of the founding leaders came from Muslim countries that were ruled by dictatorships. It is true that ISNA leaders consistently argued against dictatorships and monarchies in the Muslim world and that this was an important factor in selecting an open, democratic system, as embodied by a voting membership system. However, it would be a mistake to think this was the only factor. Many Muslim American organizations at the national, regional and local level chose different models. These other Muslim American organizations have founding leaders who came from the same countries as the ISNA leadership.

It is important to consider the vision of these founding leaders and the role of the religious nonprofit sector in the US. "[R]eligious organizations generally fit the profile of voluntary associations that involve membership and support from members . . ." In fact, membership-based organizations represent 33 percent of the nonprofit sector; when religious congregations are included, this number reaches 60 percent (Tschirhart, 2006). Therefore, to attribute ISNA's membership structure simply to the ethnicity of its founders would be a mistake; it is important to look at the complex structure of membership-based nonprofits and help situate ISNA within that subsector. ISNA's selection of a membership-based structure was largely influenced by its need for legitimacy to fulfill its vision of being the representative of the Muslim American community.

ESTABLISHING MUSLIM AMERICAN UNITY: INSTITUTIONAL COOPERATION AND COLLABORATION[4]

In 1981, a few major Muslim American organizations, which included the three groups (HSAAMs, activists and cultural pluralists), came together to establish ISNA. The new organization's purpose was to serve as an umbrella organization, one that would provide a "platform of expression" for Muslims and Islam in America.[5]

This was not the first Muslim American organization seeking to serve Islam in America. Indeed, an Islamic presence has existed in America since the 1400s. Muslim organizations in the US were focused on certain ethnic or ideological communities. However, major institutional building in the early twentieth century took place at the grassroots level, largely by the establishment of Islamic centers or organizations.[6] These institutions included ethnic and sectarian participation. In addition, organizations such as the FIA (which was established in 1952 by World War II veterans) were set up, but became less successful by the 1980s (Howell, 2010). Each of these organizations sought to meet the needs of the Muslim community in the US at that time.

The addition of a large number of Muslims from the Muslim world after

1965 dramatically changed the number and nature of Muslim Americans (Leonard, 2003, p. 10). A new organization was needed to mediate the transition of this changing Muslim American population. Initially, the MSA addressed this need. Later, this task was taken on by other organizations (for example, ISNA). The MSA initially tried to become a part of FIA, and the MSA gained sufficient memberships to secure a seat on the FIA board for many years.[7] However, by 1978, it was clear that the MSA leaders and many of its members were not comfortable with the FIA's role as a national leader.[8] It would be a mistake to assume that MSA members were completely opposed to the FIA, and *Islamic Horizons* continued to publish discussions both for and against the FIA.

A compromise among three distinctly pious, conservative Muslim American groups resulted in ISNA's founders designating it as an umbrella organization that would serve as a platform for Muslim Americans. Through ISNA, these three groups sought to develop a visible, powerful and representative national presence for Islam in America.

History had taught all three groups that it would be difficult to achieve their goals if they decided to go it alone. But utility alone did not bring these three groups together. As pious Muslims, they sought to embrace the unity that Islam called for, while simultaneously embracing the diversity it taught.

However, labeling these Muslim Americans as conservative, progressive, liberal or moderate would be a mistake. They had some basic unifying elements: all of them were religious and pious, they all embraced American ideals of democracy and pluralism, they all saw the great opportunity America presented to Islam and Muslims, and they all believed that the Islamic world was dysfunctional.

What separated them were their histories, their motivation to be a part of Islamic work and their vision for Islam in America. For example, in 1986 the ISNA *Majlis Ash-Shura* (*majlis*), or board of directors, voted to encourage Muslim Americans to engage in political and civic activities, including voting in elections. This was a historic position, but the organization's minutes noted dissenting voices within the board.[9] The fact that the final board minutes include both favorable votes and the voices of dissent suggests the compromising nature of the deliberations.

These tensions and collaborations help explain ISNA today. They also shaped immigrant and HSAAM Muslim American identity. However, we should not exaggerate the differences between these groups. After all, they were able to come together, form an organization and help it become an influential Muslim American institution, despite the fact that they recognized their diversity. As the *Islamic Horizons* editorial quoted below suggests, they probably did not realize the depth of diversity or the intricacies of their differences:[10]

A quick look at . . . Muslims . . . in North America would reveal that there are three main streams:

1. Immigrants from the Muslim countries and mainly from the Middle East and Eastern Europe who came to North America due to political and economic reasons.[11]
2. Students who are here for higher studies and many of whom stay permanently after graduation. Even for those who return home after graduation, the average length of stay is about five years.[12]
3. Native Muslims who have accepted Islam in increasing numbers in the more recent years, most of whom are Afro-Americans.[13]

Despite not fully comprehending their diversity, leaders of ISNA understood that differences existed among them and that some groups weren't represented under their umbrella.

The eventual success of the cultural pluralists pushed forward an ethnic-religious group that is on the journey of integration (not assimilation) with which America is historically familiar. However, it's vital that we know the historical journey this Muslim American identity has taken in order to understand how Muslim Americans and ISNA have evolved.

ISNA's history helps us understand not only the development of a Muslim American identity, but also gives us a window into how the transitions and confrontations related to race and ideology affected Muslim America over the past three decades. Understanding this history helps us recognize that there is no homogenous Muslim American identity. Further, the evolution of ISNA as a Muslim American nonprofit shows us the complexities that these organizations have to deal with, by virtue of attempting to gain legitimacy, both internally and externally. ISNA's history mirrors at the national level, in many ways, grassroots Muslim American civic engagement, philanthropy and ultimately institution building. ISNA's story allows us to contextualize the work of building Muslim American nonprofit organizations at a time of crisis, conflict and scrutiny.

CHAPTER OUTLINE

Chapter 1: Introduction

This introduction chapter has laid out the background to the book and offered a preliminary survey of the history of the Muslim American nonprofit sector. While situating the Muslim nonprofits in the "nonprofit" world, we have sought to tease out their Islamic identity. How Islamic education and the schools have become a part of this mix is of importance to us, as well. The introduction offered a brief literature review of the various studies and some key texts that have informed our work.

Chapter 2: Islamic Philanthropy as a Discursive Tradition

This chapter seeks to offer a theoretical framework for contextualizing Islamic philanthropy during "crisis" in the US and argues that philanthropy in this context should be seen as a gradually evolving "discursive tradition." Given the discourse of Islam in America being one framed in the rubric of crisis and the attempts by Muslim American organizations to garner philanthropic support using this framework, it is important to understand how certain crisis situations have impacted discourses of philanthropy towards this sector. This chapter attempts a Foucaldian analysis of how Muslims Americans negotiate this discursive tension in the realm of giving. We build on the work of various scholars and offer a framework that treats philanthropy towards Islamic schools and cultural and educational institutions as a "discursive tradition" to understand how the dynamics of philanthropy are changing in this sector. We propose that a genealogical approach could also offer us new insights into how philanthropy is being transformed under certain institutional constraints and relations of power.

Chapter 3: Muslim Philanthropy and Nonprofit Institutions in America

This chapter examines the history of Muslims in America with a specific focus on philanthropy and nonprofit institution building as a method of sustaining identity. This chapter reviews existing research on Muslim Americans, Islamophobia, Muslim American nonprofits and philanthropy and provides an examination of the growth and evolution of Islamic schools in America. This chapter looks at the documented presence of Muslim Americans from colonial times and asks the questions: "Why did Islam not survive beyond the first generation that it was introduced to America until this most recent migration?" and "What is the role of nonprofit institutions in sustaining Muslim American identity and religious values?"

This chapter helps lay the foundations for the importance of nonprofit institutions and philanthropy in understanding Muslim American identity and the uniquely Muslim American religious identity.

Chapter 4: Identification and Muslim American Philanthropy

The question "Who is a 'Muslim American'" is a rather complicated one. It does not yield a straight-forward answer, as one would expect. From a legal perspective, one can argue that yes, indeed, it is fairly simple: anyone with an American citizenship is an American, and if they happen to be Muslim they become Muslim American or American Muslim. But beyond this clarity lies much confusion, especially when one gets into the realm of one's "identity" as a Muslim American. We argue in this chapter that this identity is an evolution that has gained salience in a post-9/11 world. Several categories such as race, religion and ethnicity have been subsumed in this creation, and a closer examination shows that this identity is *crucial* for understanding how philanthropy occurs in the US. We build on Stuart Hall's notion of identity as a "process" to argue that the Muslim American identity is a work in progress. Finally, we offer a framework to understand the six forces that are shaping the formation of a "Muslim American" identity.

Chapter 5: Philanthropy, Institution Building and Legitimacy in Islamic Schools in America

This chapter presents the results of a national survey of full-time Islamic schools in the US and their governance practices during times of crisis (9/11 and Great Recession). There have been two prior attempts to collect national data from Islamic schools. The first was conducted by the ISNA in 1989.[14] The second data collection was by the Islamic Schools League of America (ISLA) in 2004. The survey results by ISLA have been published in a number of academic venues.

Our survey examines whether competition within the school district, greater bonding due to Islamophobia and economic stress influenced Islamic school governance practice. In addition, this chapter provides demographic data regarding Islamic schools. We draw upon existing literature on competition, Islam in America, Muslim American philanthropy, nonprofit diversity and legitimacy to examine how Islamic schools continue to navigate the challenges of Islamophobia after 9/11 followed by the economic challenges of the Great Recession of 2008. Our primary theoretical contribution is in re-examining the changing nature of philanthropy and its role in American Islamic schools. In particular, we examine how schools navigated identity, public policy and performance in search of legitimacy.

Chapter 6: Interlocutors of Tradition or Signposts of the Future of Islam in America? Islamic Schools in the US

Using data from 20 interviews with principals and board members of Islamic schools, this chapter builds a mid-range theory on how these schools have grown and the factors that have been responsible for their specific evolution in American society. While earlier studies of Islamic schools have focused on identity and curricula, we focus on organizational identity and community support for these schools, in an effort to understand and analytically frame the factors responsible for the rapid growth of such schools and what makes them unique. Using a Grounded Theory (GT) approach, we offer a theory of how these schools see themselves, their role in American societies and what strategies they have adopted to survive and thrive.

Chapter 7: Conclusion: Prospects for Future Growth and Development

The conclusion chapter draws from the various chapters from the book and offers a comprehensive overview of what is going on in the world of Islamic schools in the US. While there is a move to retain the "Islamic" in the Islamic schools, we see that there is also an increasing focus on quality, accreditation and legitimacy. While the debate about funding public schools heats up in the Trump administration, the real issues facing Islamic schools are not public funding or even vouchers, but the tension surrounding their identity factors and legitimacy. Public support of Islamic schools could become a contentious issue in the years to come with the new administration; however, it is not likely to be the key source of conflict. Islamic school leaders seem to be prioritizing leadership development, skills enhancement and networking with other institutions, to gain acceptance in the broader community as well as within the Muslim community.

NOTES

1. See "The Fear of Islam in Tennessee Public Schools," available at https://www.theatlantic.com/education/archive/2015/12/fear-islam-tennessee-public-schools/420441/ (accessed July 9, 2017).
2. This section is taken from Siddiqui (2014).
3. The first Curtis book is an invaluable primary source tool while the second is the first encyclopedia on Muslim Americans.
4. This section is taken from Siddiqui (2014).
5. ISNA Annual Report (1983).
6. For institutional building also see Haddad and Smith (1994), Abraham and Shyrock (2000), Naff (1985) and Elkholy (1966).

7. "Letter to the Editor," *Islamic Horizons*, October 1978, p. 4.
8. FIA Convention "Embarrasing and Disappointing [sic]," *Islamic Horizons*, October 1978, p. 4.
9. Meeting Minutes, ISNA Majlis Ashura, June 5, 1986.
10. "The Islamic Identity: A Myth or Reality," *Islamic Horizons*, November 1976, p. 2.
11. International activists, cultural pluralists and FIA.
12. International activists and cultural pluralists.
13. HSAAMs and other African American Muslim groups.
14. ISNA Annual Report (1990).

REFERENCES

Abraham, N. and A. Shyrock (2000), *Arab Detroit: From Margin to Mainstream*. Detroit, MI: Wayne State University Press.
Ahmed, G.M. (1991), "Muslim Organizations in the United States," in Yvonne Haddad (ed.), *The Muslims of America*. Oxford: Oxford University Press, pp. 11–24.
Cadge, W. and R. Wuthnow (2006), "Religion and the Nonprofit Sector," in Walter W. Powell and Richard Steinberg (eds.), *The Nonprofit Sector: A Research Handbook*, 2nd edn. New Haven, CT: Yale University Press, pp. 485–505.
Curtis, E.E., IV (2006), *Black Muslim Religion in the Nation of Islam*. Chapel Hill, NC: University of North Carolina Press.
Curtis, E.E., IV (2008), *The Columbia Sourcebook of Muslims in the United States*. New York: Columbia University Press.
Curtis, E.E., IV (ed.) (2010), *Encyclopedia of Muslim-American History*. New York: Facts on File.
Elkholy, A. (1966), *The Arab Moslems in the United States: Religion and Assimilation*. New Haven, CT: College & University Press.
GhaneaBassiri, K. (2010), *A History of Islam in America: From the New World to the New World Order*. New York: Cambridge University Press.
Haddad, Y. (2002), *Muslim in the West: From Sojourners to Citizens*. Oxford: Oxford University Press.
Haddad, Y. and J. Esposito (1998), *Muslims on the Americanization Path?* New York: Oxford University Press.
Haddad, Y., F. Senzai and J. Smith (2009), *Educating the Muslims of America*. New York: Oxford University Press.
Haddad, Y. and J. Smith (eds.) (1994), *Muslim Communities in North America*. Albany, NY: SUNY Press.
Hall, P.D. (2006), "A Historical Overview of Philanthropy, Voluntary Associations, and Nonprofit Organizations in the United States, 1600–2000," in Walter W. Powell and Richard Steinberg (eds.), *The Nonprofit Sector: A Research Handbook*, 2nd edn. New Haven, CT: Yale University Press, pp. 32–65.
Howell, S. (2010), "Federation of Islamic Associations of United States and Canada," in Edward E. Curtis IV (ed.), *Encyclopedia of Muslim-American History*. New York: Facts on File, p. 192–193.
Johnson, S. (1994), "The Muslims of Indianapolis," in Yvonne Haddad and Jane Smith (eds.), *Muslim Communities in North America*. New York: SUNY Press, pp. 259–278.

Khan, M. (2002), *American Muslims: Bridging Faith and Freedom*. Beltsville, MD: Amana Publications.

Leonard, K. (1997), *The South Asian Americans*. Westport, CT: Greenwood Press.

Leonard, K. (2003), *Muslims in the United States: The State of Research*. New York: Russell Sage Foundation.

Leonard, K. (2007), *Locating Home: India's Hyderabadis Abroad*. Stanford, CA: Stanford University Press.

Naff, A. (1985), *Becoming American: The Early Arab Immigrant Experience*. Carbondale, IL: Southern Illinois University Press.

Powell, W.W. and R. Steinberg (eds.) (2006), *The Nonprofit Sector: A Research Handbook*, 2nd edn. New Haven, CT: Yale University Press.

Siddiqui, S.A. (2014), *Navigating Identity through Philanthropy: A History of the Islamic Society of North America (1979–2008)*. PhD Dissertation, Indiana University.

Steinberg, R. (2006), "Economic Theories of Nonprofit Organizations," in Walter W. Powell and Richard Steinberg (eds.), *The Nonprofit Sector: A Research Handbook*, 2nd edn. New Haven, CT: Yale University Press, pp. 117–139.

Tschirhart, M. (2006), "Nonprofit Membership Associations," in Walter W. Powell and Richard Steinberg (eds.), *The Nonprofit Sector: A Research Handbook*, 2nd edn. New Haven, CT: Yale University Press, pp. 523–541.

2. Islamic philanthropy as a discursive tradition

INTRODUCTION

Speaking at the founding rally of the Organization for Afro-American Unity in 1964, Malcolm X said:

> The Organization of Afro-American Unity believes that the Afro-American community must endeavor to do the major part of all charity work from within the community. Charity, however, does not mean that to which we are legally entitled in the form of government benefits. The Afro-American veteran must be made aware of all the benefits due to him and the procedure for obtaining them.[1]

His remarks came at a time when he had broken off from the Nation of Islam (NOI), a group that was central to his development as a national leader, and joined mainstream Sunni Islam. With this move, he sought to build a self-reliant Black American Muslim community that was proud of its Black identity, as well as fully Muslim – that is, integrated in the practices and discourses of global Islam. This speech is also remarkable because it marks a shift in Malcolm X's discourse of Islam, self-identity and the role of Islam in the lives of Muslim Americans. On another level, this call he made for the community to be self-reliant meant also a growing integration with the discourses of global Islam, which he sought following his split with the NOI. Was Malcolm X dealing specifically with the issue of charity or was there an attempt to address a bigger issue of Muslim identity and community development in this instance? How have indigenous discourses of philanthropy among Black Muslims changed over a period of time?

In this chapter we seek to trace the genealogy of discourses of Islamic philanthropy among Muslim Americans, using the discourses of philanthropy among Black American Muslims and mainstream Sunni Muslims as two paradigmatic cases. We submit that through a close critical examination of the discourses of philanthropy during crisis situations, we can understand the phenomenon of how these groups seek to legitimize their work, gain followers and shape their identity. We hope to show that the discourses of philanthropy have become more "inclusive" and "liberal" over a period of time and are influenced as much by cultural dimensions and institutional constraints – governmental as well as societal – in American society, as they are by religious practices among Muslim Americans. These changes in the discourse of Islamic philanthropy have occurred in the context of a "crisis" mode, with the Muslim American community responding to challenges – both external and internal. Crisis can be understood as one of the "techniques" that have been used to frame discourses of American Islamic philanthropy. We will use a Foucaldian approach to discourse analysis in conjunction with a critical perspective advocated by James Gee (2011).

This chapter is a study of how Islamic philanthropy in the US can be understood as a constantly evolving "discursive tradition," one that has evolved and continues to evolve under the influence of other "mainstream American philanthropic discourses." The ever-changing discourses of philanthropy among the two groups I study here have been influenced by discourses of mainstream philanthropy, race, ethics, international affairs, "crisis" and community building. Primarily, my interest is to look at how crisis situations have caused a shift or discontinuity in these discourses. Foucault's advice is to look for "ruptures" or "discontinuities" in discourses as points that yield interesting insights into the transformation of discourses. By appealing to global Ummah and a transnational community, Malcolm X, like other Muslim leaders of his time, sought to legitimize his work among an international audience. Additionally, by appealing to Black identity and consciousness – through his speeches – he sought legitimacy internally in the US. A similar trend is evident in the discourses of philanthropy and community building among the most prominent Sunni Muslim group today – Islamic Society of North America (ISNA). Foucault further reminds us that discursive practices systematically "can define the objects of which they speak" (1972, p. 49). How has the discourse of philanthropy formed the American community, and how does the community form these discourses? This chapter will propose some preliminary and tentative answers.

WHAT IS A DISCURSIVE TRADITION?

Before we undertake a genealogical analysis of the discourse of philanthropy among Muslim Americans, it is imperative to understand what a "discursive tradition" is. Talal Asad, a scholar who has worked in the Foucaldian tradition, says:

> An Islamic discursive tradition is simply a tradition of Muslim discourse that addresses itself to conceptions of the Islamic past and future, with reference to

a particular Islamic practice in the present. Clearly, not everything that Muslims say and do belongs to an Islamic discursive tradition. Nor is an Islamic tradition in this sense necessarily imitative of what was done in the past. (1986, p. 14)

Our analysis of the discourses of these two large groups is based on the assumption of there being a constant evolution of discourses and practices of Islam and not an "essentialist" understanding of Islam or Muslim societies. We seek to also understand the role of tradition and reason within these discourses, and whether reason plays a public role in mediating between these discourses, as this is central to the analysis of a changing discursive tradition. Preliminary survey of the discourses of major organizations suggests that tradition is being reworked and reimagined among Muslim Americans in a very reflexive and deliberative manner. We will discuss this in later sections.

This discursive positioning of Islamic philanthropy is following the argument of Talal Asad, who has called for an anthropology of Islam that treats it as a "discursive tradition," and not an unchanging analytical concept. Asad suggests that in their representation of "Islamic tradition," Orientalists and anthropologists have ignored the role of reasoning and argument surrounding traditional practices. It is only recently that scholars have started examining the role of tradition and traditional leaders, *Ulama*, in their role in adjudicating the process of interpreting between competing discourses and using their reasoning (Zaman, 2002). Asad points to the distinction made by Abdallah Laroui, who has differentiated "tradition as structure" from "tradition as ideology." Asad further contends that the process of winning someone over to follow your traditional process involves reasoning and not just force, and is a part of Islamic discursive tradition. He says, "Power and resistance, are thus intrinsic to the development and exercise of any traditional practice." This follows from the fact that different styles of reasoning have followed different historical eras and each has fought its own battles to survive. The idea that traditions are essentially homogenous is wrong, he points out.

This approach of treating Islam as a practice-oriented religion is crucial for our argument, as it enables us to place philanthropy in the context of how Muslim Americans themselves have used it for various purposes – community building, preserving their religion and culture, and political activism. By tracing the changes of these discourses genealogically, we can understand how Muslim American organizations have understood the role of philanthropy as well as their own place in the American landscape. This is not to undermine the role of theology or interpretive practices. Orthodoxy is as relevant in this process as is orthopraxy. In the case of Islam, one can argue that one informs the other, in a dialectical process.

GhaneaBassiri (2010) has argued for understanding this development in his book *A History of Islam in America*, where he contends that the descendants of African slaves – who were often Muslims – had preserved the early Islamic traditions, which their forebears had practiced, in a form that had amalgamated both Islamic and non-Muslim traditions. He gives the example of saraka or rice cakes given by women in Georgia. The syncretic evolution of practices and, at times, paradigmatic shift in understandings of philanthropy can unpack much for us. This facet of Islamic philanthropy may offer us new perspectives when looking at Islam in America, too.

Further, we contend that since philanthropy is one of the most "American" virtues that there is, its study in the context of Muslim American non-governmental organizations (NGOs) can give us insights into how Muslim American identity is being shaped and also how Muslim American organizations are conceptualizing their role in American society. I use the changing discourses of philanthropy as articulated by ISNA and Black American Muslim groups such as the NOI and the community of Imam Warith Deen Muhammad as examples to illustrate the transformation of this discourse over a period of time, along with some recent pronouncements by the Fiqh Council of North America (FCNA). The production of discourses and knowledge about Islamic philanthropy are bound by various structures of power, as Asad reminds us. And these do not differ according to the essential character of any particular religion, but according to the "historically changing systems of discipline" (Asad, 1986, p. 5).

For practical purposes, I treat discourses within the Black American Muslim community as one group, even though there is vast divergence within them. My reason for doing this is the historical experience that most Black Americans went through and the convergence in indigenous narratives of being oppressed, being a minority and being dispossessed in a majority non-Black America. Other scholars have used a different classification of Muslim groups in America. Speaking about the various groups of Muslims, Siddiqui argues in his dissertation *Navigating Identity through Philanthropy* (2014) that:

> The Historically Sunni African American Muslims (HSAAM) movement started in the 1920s. Its members accepted traditional orthodox Islam and rejected the version of Islam being propagated by the Nation of Islam. Finally, the cultural pluralists were devout Muslims who sought to engage in building Muslim American institutions to sustain their religious identity while integrating (but not assimilating) into the structures of American society. (Siddiqui, 2014, p. 6)

ISNA would be classified as a "cultural pluralist" group by this definition.

AIM OF THE STUDY

We aim to accomplish the following primary goal through this chapter: we seek to contextualize the changing discourses about Islamic philanthropy in America and show that it continues to evolve as a "discursive tradition." How philanthropy is practiced and how discourses about it are created and managed tells us a lot about the changing dynamics within the community of practice in which these discourses are situated. We argue that a close examination of American Islamic philanthropic discourses during crisis situations can shed light on broader dimensions of how Muslim Americans make sense of aspects of belonging, community development and the like. This genealogy of Islamic philanthropy in the US also offers us a close perspective of how American Islam is evolving, in all its plurality. The dimensions of power within and outside of the community can also be examined through these discourses and one can get a sense of how these forces are shaping American Islam and Muslim American civil society.

LIMITATIONS OF THE ARGUMENT

While we examine the dominant discourses in the public sphere, what is missing is the discourse of philanthropy at the grassroots level, which is usually at the level of the mosque. GhaneaBassiri (2010) reminds us that for the "majority of non-activist Muslims, the building of mosques was a priority because it provided them with a local community through which they could socialize with other Muslims (usually of their own ethnic background) and to raise their children within an Islamic background" (p. 320). He argues that the local mosque was and is the most central Islamic institution in Muslim Americans' lives. The analysis of discourses at the local mosque level is not a part of this study, though we agree with GhaneaBassiri that it would be a worthy exercise to carry out in the near future.

BACKGROUND TO THE DEBATE

The literature review covers two sections: "Philanthropy in Crisis Situations: Role of Identity" and "Crisis in American Islam and Islamic Philanthropy." Each of these sections provides a perspective on how philanthropy in America can be understood – to substantiate the arguments made in this chapter.

PHILANTHROPY IN CRISIS SITUATIONS: ROLE OF IDENTITY

Much of the literature on philanthropy and identity is premised on what can be called "identification theory" as propounded by Paul Schervish and John Havens (2002). The identification model suggests that we give to those causes or individuals that we most directly identify with – either due to volunteering, church attendance or other related factors. Since our focus in this chapter is on religious identity, the following discussion will primarily focus on that aspect.

There is also a wide range of literature on how religious identity does or does not impact giving. Bekkers and Weipking (2011) have identified eight mechanisms as the most important forces that drive giving: (1) awareness of need, (2) solicitation, (3) costs and benefits, (4) altruism, (5) reputation, (6) psychological benefits, (7) values and (8) efficacy. While awareness and values form two important parts of this spectrum, they are not the primary ones. They further argue that "Religious beliefs have rarely been analyzed in relation to philanthropy. Davidson and Pyle (1994) find that more orthodox and stronger religious beliefs are positively related to religious contributions, but this relationship is mediated by church attendance." This gap in the literature is important. Apart from these factors, they mention studies by Brooks (2005), which demonstrated that religious attendance is negatively correlated with giving to secular causes, and other studies which showed that giving to human services was in no way related to religious affiliation (Marx, 2000).

Philanthropy and crisis situations are intimately connected, especially in our hyper-technology-driven world, with online and text giving making giving easy and quick. But let us first clarify what we mean by a "crisis." Boin et al. (2005) define a crisis as: "A serious threat to the system when the basic values and norms, which under time pressure and uncertain circumstances necessitate timely decision making" (p. 2). Crisis situations are further divided into man made, natural or acts of God. These days, there is also the added dimension of technological crises. Similarly, as Jonathan Benthall and Jérôme Bellion-Jourdan have argued in their book *The Charitable Crescent* (2003), the global humanitarian movement in and towards the Muslim world is a somewhat new phenomenon, and is not as old as that in the Western world, which pioneered it in the model of Red Cross. But this is not to say that the notion of charity among Muslims is new. Benthall and Bellion-Jourdan point to the diversity of objectives among NGOs working in the relief and reconstruction efforts in Iraq and say:

Those charged with regulating relief and reconstruction in Iraq need to bear in mind both the diversity of objectives that Islamic charities bring to bear and the diversity of their funding sources. Some are awash with Gulf States' oil, while others represent the fruits of zakat contributions from all Muslims around the world and what has been described as the "philanthropy of the poor." There is also a case to be made for the businesses to get involved, as in the case of Mecca Cola, which can mobilize the *Ummah*. (p. 10)

Benthall and Bellion-Jourdan are referring to the often monolithic discourse about any sort of funding that goes to the Muslim world and the tendency to club all forms of giving together with that which supports spurious and extremist activities. While support for militant groups did occur during armed conflicts such as Bosnia and the Soviet occupation of Afghanistan amongst others, the trend seems to be more towards humanitarian giving. We must pay attention to the latter, as much or perhaps more than the former, as it forms a significant part of global giving, Benthall and Bellion-Jourdan point out. Further, Benthall (2008) makes a claim that all giving is political in nature. He makes this argument on the basis of the history of transnational aid from Muslim organizations. We believe that runs counter to the ethos of giving and that there is greater evidence for the contrary view that philanthropy is more than politics. Peter Frumkin (2006) argues for this position that giving reflects not just political action, but is more than that. In combining one's vision and values, philanthropy is an expression of a bigger vision of one's life and cannot be considered only as political. Especially, looking at it from a donor's perspective, it would be wrong to assume that the only thing that donors are interested in is influencing some political outcome or policy. Donors are motivated by a range of ideas, visions and emotions all of which could be considered as trying to make the world a better place.

When a major humanitarian disaster strikes, there is a greater awareness of need and a consequent drive to generate support for the cause, both financial and material, resulting in enhanced fundraising efforts. Bekkers and Weipking (2011) have argued that this "awareness of need" is a critical component of the success of a philanthropic effort. With greater awareness of need, through media campaigns, the internet and social media outreach, a greater number of people are being mobilized for activism and fundraising.

When a major disaster (tsunami for instance) strikes, philanthropy tends to go up, as various reports and empirical studies have shown (Giving USA, 2013; Hudson Institute, 2012). While a variety of knee-jerk reactions take place, primarily one can divide the challenges of managing a crisis into various steps. The leaders of humanitarian NGOs face five tasks, as Boin et al. have argued. They say that crisis leadership is a complex process that brings together various challenges that require different skills. "Crisis leadership then involves five critical tasks: sense making, decision making, meaning making, terminating, and learning" (Boin et al., 2005). While they are dealing with the various aspects of sense making, including that of their own care values, the conclusions they reach can have profound implications on how they understand their own selves and their communities. With globalization, increased contact with others, and greater opportunities to understand and interact with others, we believe the chances for identity expansion are greater than identity contraction, especially in a crisis situation.

CRISIS IN AMERICAN ISLAM AND ISLAMIC PHILANTHROPY

Islam in America has been framed as being in a state of "crisis" by many Muslim American leaders. While they are not referring to an existentialist threat to Americans, the references are to a more ethical and spiritual crisis, with increasing materialism, degradation of moral values in the public sphere and so on. So, are Muslim Americans facing what Alisdair MacIntyre called an "epistemological crisis"? What are the dimensions and how does one make sense of such a "crisis" and its impact on how people come together to help one another – a manifestation of philanthropic behavior?

MacIntyre writes in his essay "Epistemological Crises, Dramatic Narrative and the Philosophy of Science" (1977) that an epistemological crisis is one that changes all rules of the game, according to which we understand reality. Using the example of Shakespeare's Hamlet, he says "Hamlet arrives back from Wittenberg with too many schemata available for interpreting the events at Elsinore of which already he is a part. There is the revenge schema of the Norse sagas; there is the renaissance courtier's schema; there is a Machiavellian schema about competition for power." So, in effect, on Hamlet's return he is faced with an "epistemological crisis" of answering the question "what is going on here"? Further, McIntyre argues, "Hamlet's problems arise because the dramatic narrative of his family and of the kingdom of Denmark through which he identified his own place in society and his relationships to others has been disrupted by radical interpretative doubts." As Hamlet tries to make sense of this new reality and narrative, there is a struggle to understand the changed scenario and an attempt made to adjust according to it.

The way around this crisis is the construction of a new narrative. MacIntyre says, "When an epistemological crisis is resolved, it is by the construction of a new narrative which enables the agent to understand both how he or she could intelligibly have held his or her original beliefs and how he or she could have been so drastically misled by them" (p. 455). Is it possible to understand the narratives of Muslim American philanthropy in the US through the examination of the discourses of crisis?

The history of Muslim Americans and Islam in America is steeped in a discourse of crises of various sorts. Whether it is the subaltern philanthropy of former slaves in Antebellum America which GhaneaBassiri alludes to (GhaneaBassiri, 2010) or that of the post-9/11 narrative of "Muslim American philanthropy in decline" which many organizations claimed (Jamal, 2011), there is a constant reference to the changed rules of the game and a deeply felt inability on the part of the agents involved to understand "what is going on." This radical shaking up of one's assumptions about the world is accompanied by the search for a new narrative. As GhaneaBassiri suggests and other scholars have argued, this search led to early Muslim Americans trying to find common ground with their co-religionists. This meant creating discourses of giving and philanthropy that incorporated elements from their ancestral traditions and also discourses in contemporary American society. Tariq Ramadhan has also argued that Western Muslims are in a state of flux, caught between "modernity and Islam," since modernity is based on a distrust of tradition, if not direct opposition (2001, p. 5). Though there is a recognition of the need for scholars and thinkers to move beyond this framing of Islam versus the West, currently this mode of thinking dominates public as well as scholarly discourses about Islam in the West.

In a similar vein, Sheikh Hamza Yusuf, one of the most prominent and well-known Islamic scholars in the US, recently spoke to a group of Muslim American community leaders about Imam Ghazali, the twelfth century scholar, considered one of the greatest Islamic jurists and theologians. In a meeting in Kentucky, he said that Imam Ghazali's life reminds us not to squander our lives in gratuitous frivolity. Ghazali said that all paths of our lives lead to death, but only a few lead to a good death. Before we die, it is our responsibility to live as people of *Ihsan*, or mercy, those whose presence made a positive contribution to the world. He further added:

> I would argue that we are in the greatest crisis we have been in, as a community
> – us Muslims – and I will conclude that by saying why Imam Ghazali is important today. He hated sectarianism, one that was provincial. It was trapped in the realm of particulars and incapable of seeing universals. He also understood the concept of wayfarers.[2]

Sheikh Yusuf goes on to say that in times such as these, we need Muslims who are transformative in nature. We need Muslims who will not only constantly work to transform their souls to be better humans each day, but also bring peace and purity to the world. What did Sheikh Yusuf mean by "crisis"? Is this rubric useful to understand how Muslims in the US comprehend their own situation? I suggest that crisis can be seen as a "technique" or "technology" in a Foucaldian sense. This way of looking at Islamic philanthropy is theoretically and practically useful, as Foucault suggests. Similarly, this "crisis" framing follows the criticism of an anthropology of Islam that Asad says is not very useful for analyzing Muslim societies. Asad argues that much of the anthropology of Islam is situated in a "dramatic struggle" of sorts that scholars such as Gellner and Geertz have talked about. This narrative excludes other analytical points, such as integration of ideas, norms and so on. Also, with this narrative of "turning all Islamic behavior into readable gesture," much nuance is lost (Asad, 1986, p. 9). Asad's point of considering historical conditions that produce a given situation for a community or tribe is key. He also advocates considering the historical roots of indigenous discourses in any community under study.

The discourse of Islam being in crisis is not new. The Black Nationalist movement, with the NOI as one of its key organizations, also used this discourse in the 1960s; so did the mainstream Muslim American organizations such as the ISNA in the 1970s and 1980s. Speaking of the founding of ISNA in Indianapolis in 1981, Siddiqui (2014) argues that the educational mission of the organization took precedence over other aspects. So, in effect, the mission of ISNA was seen as providing Islamic education to Muslim Americans. He further adds:

> MSA's leaders considered educating Muslim Americans about Islam an important first step. The next step in their view was to translate this educational mission into an Islamic identity rather than a cultural one. In addition, MSA sought to build upon the revival of Islam in the aftermath of the Iranian revolution. In their view, these religious values needed to inform Muslim American political advocacy. (p. 56)

This movement in values and discourse was taking place in the context of international engagement by ISNA leaders as well as domestic changes in rhetoric and discourse about Islam. The reason that ISNA came into being was because Muslims in America felt that their children were not learning "authentic" Islam and that there was a danger of them losing their faith.

If one looks beyond the 1980s and closer to our times, the biggest crisis that Muslim Americans faced was in 2001, with the September 11 attacks which radically changed how Islam was perceived in the US (Haddad and Harb, 2014). As Haddad and Harb argue,

> The increase in hostility toward Islam and Muslims by security officials appears to have a direct impact on the faith and practice of Islam in the U.S., including the interpretation of the tenets and scriptures of the faith, the formation of Muslim identity in America, and the emphasis on volunteerism and civic engagement. For many Muslims and those who study the religion, Islam in America since 9/11 has undergone significant transformations. (p. 478)

They contend that in a post-9/11 world, most Muslim Americans are adopting a discourse of American Islam that is sensitive to the needs of the population. Further, they say that the transformation of American Islam is taking place and this sometimes coincides with the objectives of US policy. What they seem to be implying through their article is that the crisis of 9/11 had an impact on the discourse of Islam in America and how Americans themselves responded to the challenges placed before them.

The crisis that Sheikh Yusuf alluded to in his speeches, and one that is often invoked, is a crisis in terms of both identity and knowledge. Similarly, ISNA was set up to form an "authentically grounded Islamic sphere" according to Siddiqui. This was because "ISNA's founders took the view that 'authentic' Islam had not survived in America because of the lack of theologically grounded Islamic institutions. They wanted to ensure the establishment and sustenance of mainstream Islam – one developed through education and learning, rather than through compromise" (2014, p. 63). The need to build institutions that would preserve "authentic Islam" is one of the key reasons why ISNA came about. Other organizations such as the Muslim Public Affairs Council (MPAC) and the Council on American–Islamic Relations (CAIR) are similarly guided by the need to build an authentic Muslim community, though their missions are slightly broader (Haddad and Harb, 2014).

Speaking of the crisis of knowledge that Muslims in general face, Sheikh Yusuf says: "Our epistemology is different from that of the current dominant model in the world. If we just go to current universities, without critically analyzing this difference, we become victims of this knowledge." If we don't know the methodologies and epistemologies, and understand how we know "Truth," we compound our knowledge. He argues that people are being taught the wrong approach to knowledge in ignoring God as the source of all. He further adds that if we don't see that we have lost our metaphysical grounding in the Muslim Ummah, we will be trapped in the economic and social causes – we will miss out on the spiritual crisis.

The spiritual crisis that Hamza Yusuf and other religious scholars speak of seems real to many organizations and individuals, who are articulating their discourse of philanthropy and community building in these terms. In the following sections, we will examine these discourses more closely. It is also worth noting that this speech was given as a fundraiser for Zaytuna

College, which was founded by Sheikh Hamza Yusuf, and he argues that the current crisis of knowledge can be addressed by institutions such as Zaytuna College, which offer a balance of reason and spiritual knowledge, a tension we will explore later in this chapter.

SAMPLE

We compare the changing discourse of philanthropy towards education/educational institutions among two large groups of Muslim Americans – the Black Muslims represented by Imam Warith Deen Muhammad and "cultural pluralists" represented by ISNA, the largest membership-based group of Muslims in North America. The Black Muslims comprise over one-third of the Muslim American population by some estimates (GhaneaBassiri, 2010). As the forebears of Islam in America, they are considered more "legitimate" inheritors of the Islamic leadership in America by some, while the "immigrant" Muslims, who primarily came from Asia and the Middle East following the Immigration Reform Act of 1965, are considered new Americans. There is tension between the two groups, as we will examine later in this chapter.

DATA COLLECTION METHODS

We will use a variety of resources for the project that we undertake in this chapter. We will use a variety of existing primary and secondary resources that will help us map the changing discourses of philanthropy in the organizations under study. Some of the sample documents that will be helpful include:

- Historical data including speeches
- Websites of organizations
- Dissertations or books about the organizations and key personalities
- Biographical information about key personalities that may be relevant to our research questions.

FINDINGS AND DISCUSSION

Crises are key to understanding how philanthropic discourses in the Muslim American community transformed. We argue that each of these crises offer us what Hermann et al. (1987) have called Occasions for Decision (OFD), during which the Muslim American community responded in different ways. We will trace the changing discourses of philanthropy among the Black Muslims and the mainstream Sunni Muslims, as two paradigmatic groups, to map the genealogy of the discourse.

In the next section, we will briefly describe how each event was perceived by the Black Americans and the mainstream Sunni Muslims and examine the change of discourses in each group separately. Our attempt goes beyond a purely "dramatic narrative" of events and actors, and looks at the analytical import of what occurred. This strategy is key if we are to avoid "essentializing" about groups or communities, as Asad has argued (Asad, 1986). This also implies that historical and other forces acting on the events are of equal import, besides the belief system of these groups. The political economy, history of internal discourses, and power relations with the government and other social groups all become important in this perspective.

The key events that are of interest to our research are:

1.   The First Gulf War of 1990
2.   The attacks of September 11, 2001.

We chose these two events as they represent moments of deep concern and anxiety as well as a lack of internal cohesion and discord within the Muslim community. The reactions of each of these groups was varied, and within the groups there were various interpretations of how best to react to the situations. They were no doubt very significant events, both in terms of the scale of the event itself and also the import they had, for how Muslims were perceived in the US after they occurred. They could be considered "crises" under the definition of Boin et al. discussed earlier. Further, these two events represent a deep involvement of Muslim Americans in political activism in the US, as GhaneaBassiri (2010) has argued. He suggests that post the Iranian Revolution, Muslim Americans had started to get increasingly involved in the political life of America, hoping to influence the ethical framework of American political and social life. Siddiqui (2014) argues that this was a result of the choices placed before the community at large – whether to be isolationists or to get actively involved in the public and political life of the US. Most American organizations chose the latter, he contends.

GhaneaBassiri suggests that many leaders such as Abdul Rauf saw Islam as offering an ethical tradition and an alternative to the capitalist model in place. GhaneaBassiri suggests that despite calls for unity during the 1950s and 1960s, there was no great urgency to "unite" in America, as the disunity did not threaten their existence. But these events, as we will see, challenged this assumption.

Let us look at each in turn and briefly examine how discourses of Islamic philanthropy changed as a result of the crisis.

1. First Gulf War of 1990

The First Gulf War was a key moment for Muslim Americans, as it was a moment when Muslim Americans were able to assert their voice. Though there were differing interpretations of how the US and Muslim Americans should react to this aggression by Saddam Hussein against Kuwait, the reaction by each of the groups examined here was quite different.

The grassroots Muslim sentiment did not support American intervention in the Middle East, as these interventions were seen as being politically driven and not in the best interest of the people in those countries. ISNA decided to side with the broader grassroots sentiment among Muslim Americans that opposed any intervention, in effect incurring the wrath of its Gulf donors, who wanted the Muslim Americans to lobby their government for intervention, argues Siddiqui (2014). He further says:

> At a time when ISNA desperately needed funding, it had to choose between endorsing American intervention in the war, as supported by its Gulf donors, and siding with Muslim Americans' opposition to such intervention. In so doing, ISNA had to choose between pragmatism and idealism. ISNA stayed true to its values and its Muslim American constituents by opposing American military involvement in this conflict. In the short run, this decision further devastated the organization's financial situation. (p. 105)

However, in the long run, this long-term support of the grassroots is what made the organization the leading voice for Muslim Americans, argues Siddiqui. Similarly, GhaneaBassiri (2010) points to the historical background for why Muslims reacted negatively to American intervention in the war. While they appreciated Saddam's support of Palestine, there was an awareness about the hypocrisy of Saddam's effort to Islamize Iraq, he says. Further, groups such as ISNA saw through the efforts of the US to reinforce its hegemony in the Middle East by way of this war, calling for the US to re-evaluate its policies in the region. This debate is still ongoing, with most "grassroots" Muslims opposing any American intervention in the Middle East for ethical reasons.

The reaction by the Black Muslims, as represented by Imam Warith Deen Muhammad, was quite the opposite, as he sought to support the war efforts. Siddiqui quotes him as saying

> We have Islamic interest first, and then other interests come second, not before Islamic interests. . . . I am comfortable with the decision which Saudi Arabia has taken to defend its borders and to accept the support of its friends – not only

America but other friends, Muslim nations and non-Muslim friendly nations. (pp. 111–112)

What did Imam Warith Deen Muhammad mean by "Islamic interests"? Was he referring to a global Islamic identity or one specific to his group? Putting his quote in context, one can see that he was using a global framing of Islam and Muslims. While doing so, he also asserted the rights of Saudi Arabia to align with its regional allies, in an effort to garner support to do what was right in its best interests. Also, by making the discourse about "Islam," and not any nation-states, he seems to have consciously framed the debate around higher moral principles rather than national interests. One should also further note that Saudi Arabia houses the holiest places of Islam – Mecca and Medina – and hence this framing could potentially have been made to appeal to the religious authority of Saudi Arabia, to gain legitimacy for the country's actions. GhaneaBassiri quotes Yvonne Haddad as saying that Imam Warith Deen Muhammad was the only Muslim leader of significance who endorsed the American war in Iraq. This is significant in itself, and occurred, according to Haddad, as Imam Warith Deen Muhammad wanted to assure the Saudis and Kuwaitis that the US is not at war against Islam.

Siddiqui contends that there was a differing interpretation of how philanthropy and philanthropic support towards their organizations would be affected by this public position. While ISNA paid a heavy (though short-term) price for opposing the war, Imam Warith Deen Muhammad sought to gain legitimacy as well as philanthropic support for his causes through this public support of the First Gulf War. While this could be seen as a purely pragmatic attempt to gain legitimacy, Imam Warith Deen Muhammad's earlier position on American foreign policy and Muslims participation in wars seems to be a more moral stand. In response to a question from a Muslim about whether Muslims should participate in wars to defend America's foreign policy, he is reported to have said "I think a citizen, a good citizen, would feel himself threatened by any attacks from outside or from inside. It's nothing but common sense for us to lend our support to our nation against those things that seek to weaken, undermine or destroy it" (Siddiqui, 2014). But he also goes on to say that this decision should be made by each individual and it is not right for any organization to tell them what to do.

The shift from this earlier position in 1981 to a more hardline one supporting America's active intervention can be seen as a change in discourse of the Black American movement, especially that of Imam Warith Deen Muhammad, to gain a wider legitimacy within the Muslim world. While other groups such as the NOI remained on the fringes of the Muslim American movements, Imam Warith Deen Muhammad sought to actively integrate Black American Muslims both with the American mainstream and with the wider Muslim world.

The key shift in the Black American community has been the move from radical Black Nationalism towards a softer, mainstream or orthodox Muslim identity. GhaneaBassiri argues that as the African Americans' lot gradually improved, the separatist, nationalist ideology of the NOI was toned down and finally eliminated when Imam Warith Deen Muhammad turned it into a Sunni organization in 1975–76. While this was not an entirely easy process, since giving up the NOI's racist rhetoric also meant giving up its core identity, the process seems to have been all but completed. While the Black Muslims sought legitimacy and philanthropic support from international organizations, ISNA sought legitimacy and financial support from the local Muslim American community. We will examine how their respective discourses sought to accomplish this.

2. September 11, 2001 and its Aftermath

Several scholars have written thoughtfully about the attacks of September 11, 2001 and its impact on Muslim Americans (GhaneaBassiri, 2010; Esposito and Kalin, 2011; Safi, 2003; Ernst, 2003). While there is widespread agreement that this act, in effect, brought about a great amount of Islamophobia and greater misrepresentation about Islam in the public sphere, it is not often seen as the event that also altered how Islamic philanthropy is perceived in the US post 9/11. The events of 9/11 led to the passing of the USA PATRIOT Act, which gave sweeping powers to various agencies of the US to crack down on any activities that were deemed harmful to the American national interests. This included clamping down on organizations that provided "material support" to terrorist groups or individuals, anywhere in the world. This led, these scholars suggest, to not only a curtailment of civil liberties, but also a clamping down on several Muslim NGOs that functioned for several years, carrying out work both domestically and internationally (Haddad and Harb, 2014; Singer, 2008; Alterman and von Hippel, 2007).

While ISNA and its member organizations sought to control the damage done to the image of Islam and Muslims in general, they also released certain fatwas (religious rulings). One such example drew parallels between the Qur'anic injunctions about the sanctity of life and how the terrorists who attacked the twin towers had violated it. This fatwa also reminded Muslims that any attack on a civilian can be considered unlawful and should not receive any support from righteous Muslims. This fatwa was signed by many prominent leaders who were part of ISNA. More than 145 Muslim organizations endorsed this fatwa.

On the other hand, the government of the US sought to limit the damage to US national security through the passage of the PATRIOT Act; many scholars and thinkers have pointed out that this had serious effects on how philanthropy towards Muslim institutions was perceived (Jamal, 2011).

While the attacks of 9/11 brought on a renewed interest in studying radical Islam and the dangers it posed to America, it did not "change everything" for Muslim Americans, argues scholar of American Islam, Edward Curtis IV. He says:

> For much of the twentieth century, it was not Muslim immigrants, but rather indigenous African American Muslims who were, from the point of view of federal authorities, the public and potentially dangerous face of American Islam. The parallels between earlier and later periods of state surveillance are striking. We seem to be living in a new age of consensus in which, like the late 1940s and 1950s, a vital center has identified Islamic radicalism, and by extension Muslim American dissent, as an existential problem, a dangerous expression of extremism.[3]

Curtis is arguing for looking back at American history, particularly with the growth of the NOI and other nationalist movements that were clearly seen as a threat to American sovereignty. The incidents of 9/11 further compounded the discourse of "Good Muslim, bad Muslim" say Haddad and Harb (2014). This notion, borrowed from the famous book *Good Muslim, Bad Muslim* by Mahmood Mamdani, argues that the "moderate Muslims" are to be cultivated while "extremists" are to be treated with suspicion and are a clear threat to the US and much of the Western world. What has shifted, according to Curtis, is the perception of fear. In the 1940s and 1950s it was the Black Muslims who were the object of fear and surveillance and now it is the Brown Muslims, he contends. There is also a conflation of various discourses of national security, religion, secularism and Islamic norms of philanthropy when one speaks of the tragic events of 9/11.

Curtis further reminds us that while the fear of the NOI among the American establishment diminished, the post-Cold War fears of Islamic radicalism sweeping through and opposing American interests both at home and abroad were real. He says that Presidents George W. Bush and Barak Obama sought to reconcile with Islam, as they could not afford to keep up the rhetoric of "Clash of civilizations."

> They attempted to incorporate and co-opt Islam in the name of U.S. interests. "Islam is peace," declared George W. Bush on September 17, 2001. "Muslims make an incredibly valuable contribution to our country," he said. Similarly, Barack Obama proclaimed in his 2009 address in Cairo that "Islam has always been a part of America's story." Rather than reject Islam outright, both presidents attempted to legitimize forms of Islam that were either apolitical or seemingly pro-American.[4]

This is an interesting analytical point for our discussion. The co-optation of the discourse of "Islam as a religion of peace" by the American government is a useful dynamic to observe. Further, one must also note that Obama chose this occasion to remind his audience in Cairo that the US government would take all steps to ensure that Muslim Americans can pay their zakat, with ease. He said:

> Freedom of religion is central to the ability of peoples to live together. We must always examine the ways in which we protect it. For instance, in the United States, rules on charitable giving have made it harder for Muslims to fulfill their religious obligation. That's why I'm committed to working with American Muslims to ensure that they can fulfill zakat.[5]

One could analyze this speech in much depth, as it was pegged as a "new beginning" with the Middle East. Why did he have to do this, in a foreign country, to an audience who were not voting for him? One can see that this was partly to win the public relations battle, post George W. Bush's era, where Mr. Bush had been seen as a "crusader" against Islam. Further, one can perhaps see the logic of his remarks in trying to address domestic concerns of Muslims in America – who were fearful that the administration was against them. This was a discursive strategy, which was aimed at both domestic and foreign audiences.

While Muslim Americans were reeling from the shock of the attacks of 9/11 and trying to make sense of what had just occurred, this shift in the establishment discourse towards Islam did help, at least momentarily. But as we see, immediately following the passage of the PATRIOT Act, and after Executive Order 13224 and anti-terrorist funding guidelines from the Treasury Department, there was a strong reaction towards the Muslim philanthropic sector. Zahra Jamal, in her policy report titled *Ten Years after 9/11* for the Washington DC think tank the Institute for Social Policy and Understanding (ISPU), suggests that there was up to a 50 percent drop in donations to Muslim humanitarian relief organizations post 9/11. Echoing similar sentiments, Curtis says that "Muslim American charities that provided non-military aid to organizations designated as terrorist groups, such as the Palestinian party Hamas, were raided and shut down."[6] The discourse around Islamic philanthropy at this time became couched in the "war on terror" and had negative connotations throughout this period. Muslim American organizations sought to distance themselves from those entities and militant ideologies that had brought about these violent acts, but the after effects of this violent act lingers, as the Treasury Department has come up with new guidelines for those wanting to support organizations and individuals in "troubled spots" from an ethical or humanitarian perspective. The discourse of Islamic philanthropy that the Treasury

Department has used since 9/11 has not changed much, and one can see how public policies made with this framing have had a deleterious impact on how Islamic philanthropy is perceived in policy circles.

ISNA'S TURN FROM PAROCHIALISM TO "CULTURAL PLURALISM"

Siddiqui (2014) argues that President Obama's opening statement during his inaugural address on January 20, 2009 that the US today is a "nation of Christians and Muslims, Hindus and Jews," with the president of ISNA, Ingrid Mattson, present, is a significant landmark in the Muslim American community's history. Siddiqui contends that ISNA has had to embrace a broad identity, of being "cultural pluralists", as it had to gain legitimacy within the Muslim American community, which is incredibly diverse. "Because of the incredible diversity within the Muslim American community, ISNA needed to embrace a broad identity for internal legitimacy. This internal legitimacy was vital in order to counter the Islamophobia that impeded external legitimacy," he adds (p. 4). This move towards embracing cultural pluralism could be seen as pragmatic, as well as an effort to consciously reinterpret notions of diversity within Islam, which seek to honor diversity of opinion.

One can also see how the moves by ISNA leaders to try to win their intellectual freedom during crisis points such as the First Gulf War and subsequent incidents helped win a strong base of support. This positioning of the organization is key for understanding how ISNA navigated differences. ISNA used a combination of both religious and practical, organizational discourses to justify its stand in this instance. The original positioning of ISNA in the 1950s and 1960s was of an organization that was ambiguous about the concept of a "Muslim American" identity. One can argue that it possibly did not exist, as many of the students and young professionals who were part of the Muslim Student Association (MSA) – the precursor to ISNA – were of immigrant origin and imagined going back to their home countries after their education in the US was complete. Many did; however, those who stayed back and found jobs in the US did not imagine living here successfully. It took several decades for a "Muslim American consciousness" to emerge among this group, and ISNA was among the first to make a progressive shift towards integration, if not assimilation into the American social fabric.

Following the successful annual convention in 1997, when more than 21 000 Muslim Americans showed up, Siddiqui says: "The fact that the organization did not represent all of the Muslim American community, particularly a large number of African-American Muslims, did not deter the leaders of ISNA to declare success" (p. 135). This has been possible because of the moral and practical legitimacy that ISNA enjoys, argues Siddiqui.

BLACK MUSLIMS: FROM ISOLATIONISM TO INTEGRATION

The NOI was one of the most prominent and powerful Muslim American groups in the 1950s and 1960s. The NOI sought to create a uniquely Black identity, and it also co-opted notions of "mainstream" Islam, that is, Sunni Islam for its own legitimacy. While several of its core beliefs were contradictory to mainstream "authentic" Sunni or Shii Islam, its leaders sought to gain legitimacy for the organization and its message by aligning with other Muslim groups internationally and by also how they positioned organizational discourse regarding race, self-reliance and philanthropy.

Race, ethnicity, religion and philanthropy have come together histori-cally in the discourse of American Islam. As Sherman Jackson reminds us, though some scholars and activists argue that Islam does not "do race," Islam does "do reality." In dealing with the practical realities of race relations in the US, Muslim Americans come face to face with their own deeply held misconceptions and prejudices, he argues (Jackson, 2008). Further, Jackson challenges the dominant discourse of Islam among immi-grant Muslims, who assume that the mental frameworks and models that they bring – that are rooted in the realities of Muslim lands – are treated as primary objects of Muslim religious contemplation, while ignoring the Black American contexts. As he further argues, the role of Sunni Islam offers the Black American Sunni Islam a model to emulate in terms of a discourse of intellectual tradition. "The point, in other words, is not to go back in search of cut-and-dried solutions but to benefit from tradition's authority and intellectual capital, while heightening the likelihood that one's own deliberations are not derailed by the allure of undisciplined compromise or crass, 'religionized pragmatism'" (Jackson, 2008, p. 4).

The Prophet's last sermon is often cited as an authoritative text for claiming that Islam does not "do race," but Jackson argues that even if in principle this is true, practical realities in America and other parts of the world dictate that we be sensitive to the idea of racial hatred and its ugly manifestation. The following passage from the Prophet's last sermon is illustrative of this idea:

All mankind is from Adam and Eve, an Arab has no superiority over a non-Arab nor a non-Arab has any superiority over an Arab; also a white has no superiority over black nor does a black have any superiority over white except by piety and good action. Learn that every Muslim is a brother to every Muslim and that the Muslims constitute one brotherhood. Nothing shall be legitimate to a Muslim which belongs to a fellow Muslim unless it was given freely and willingly. Do not, therefore, do injustice to yourselves. (Source: Islamicity.com)

While this passage and its meaning have been used to create this race-neutral discourse, at various points in Muslim American history, Muslims themselves have sought to create counter-discourses that have sought to legitimize their position in the US based on their race. As GhaneaBassiri shows in his book *A History of Islam in America* (2010), one of the most egregious forms of discrimination against Muslims or "Oriental" immigrants in the early eighteenth century was in the area of naturalization. These groups were not allowed to purchase land and the Naturalization Act of 1790 granted citizenship only to "aliens being free white persons." This further changed to "aliens of African nativity and to persons of African descent" in 1870, and it took more than a century for Muslims to get full rights to citizenship. GhaneaBassiri says, "In response to legal challenges to their eligibility for American citizenship, both Syrians and Indians relied on contemporary ethnological classifications of race to define themselves as white" (p. 153). There were various attempts to claim this proximity between the immigrants' racial identity and those of the dominant white race in America. Religion played a part in this process contends GhaneaBassiri, since Syrians and others presented themselves as a racial category and not necessarily a religious category. The "Muslim" identity of many of these people was either played down or kept a secret. GhaneaBassiri further argues that in this phase, ethnicity played a far greater role than did religion in how Muslim Americans articulated their demands for inclusion on the national stage. They also formed self-help associations to organize their efforts and counter the government's challenges to their rights as US citizens.

The gradual shift from isolationism to integration with mainstream "Sunni Islam" can be seen as a confluence of various forces – both domestic and international. GhaneaBassiri suggests that this move occurred as the American state started to downgrade the importance with which it saw the NOI. But we would suggest that perhaps a combination of factors, such as the death of Malcolm X, efforts by Imam Warith Deen Muhammad to join mainstream Islam and his message to his followers to break from the racist ideologies of the Nation, and growing internationalization of American Islam, contributed to the Black American Muslim leaders recognizing that there is a need for greater collaboration and integration with discourses at the international level. The growing influence of petro-dollars as a source of revenue for Muslim American groups should also not be discounted. As the Saudis and Kuwaitis started to send missionaries and to fund mosques and other institutions in the US, they sought allies who would stand by their messaging, GhaneaBassiri seems to suggest.

As Siddiqui argues,

> Another important overture was to reach out to Farrakhan and the Nation of Islam. Many within ISNA considered believers of the Nation of Islam to be heretical and non-Muslims. By the late 1990s, Farrakhan started making overtures to ISNA. He hired a Sunni Imam, Shaikh Tijani, as an advisor. Ahmed ElHattab was assigned to serve as liaison between Farrakhan and ISNA. (2014, p. 157)

Despite Farrakhan's conversion to Sunni Islam in 2000, there wasn't much progress towards reconciling the differences between ISNA and the NOI. Siddiqui also suggests that the efforts on the part of ISNA to help Imam Warith Deen Muhammad to set up an organization, as he was just a spiritual leader without an organizational structure, failed.

REASON AS A DISCURSIVE STRATEGIC TOOL?

In the foregoing discussion, we have examined how institutions reacted to external circumstances, in order to legitimize their work, survive crisis situations and build credibility. What is missing thus far is the role of religion, religious authorities and interpretive paradigms that have transformed Islamic philanthropy into what it is today. We argue that while the religious norms of Islamic philanthropy in the US are derived from the Qur'an and Hadith, and thus remain unchanged, the day-to-day practice of Islamic philanthropy is guided by pragmatic considerations and also new ways of interpreting the religious requirements. This is a manifestation of the "discursive tradition" that Asad (1986) speaks of.

There is a tension between how religious norms are interpreted by religious leaders and how they are practically implemented, at the organizational or individual level. The great debates in Islamic philosophy – both classical as well as contemporary – have been about the ethics of religion and whether they are subjective or objective. As Olive Leaman (1985) contends, "A great deal of the Muslim establishment – Shaifii, Hanbal, Al-Ashari, and a large number of other theologians and jurists, firmly lined up on the side of tradition, believing that any other position would deny God's power" (p. 147). Leaman adds that according to these scholars this also implies that if we could determine God's will, then could we not then form an independent view of what is right and wrong. The notion of independent thought has been argued as forming a slippery slope to being unfaithful. Further, traditionalists have argued that this independence takes us away from the certainty of faith and belief, which is embodied in revelation.

This point is relevant in our discussion of Islamic philanthropy, as it is guided by scriptural and religious norms as well as secular understandings. For instance, the Qur'an mandates zakat to be spent on eight categories of people, and the rest are not deserving of zakat, while sadaqa can be given to anyone, Muslim or non-Muslim; the debate about who falls into the categories is at the heart of many discussions. The recent development of the humanitarian aid movement in the Muslim world is an indicator of the growing felt need for charity. Can zakat be given to non-Muslims? This question has vexed and continues to bother those in the nonprofit sector, who may have missions that align them to serve the needs of not just Muslims, but everyone. Further, government regulations and administrative policies in international NGOs stipulate non-discrimination. How do Muslim American NGOs deal with such situations? Such instances can call for not only creative reinterpretation of the rules of zakat, but also for greater validation from religious authorities, so donors can actually donate to these organizations without feeling that they have donated to an organization that does not follow Islamic norms of zakat distribution. To address these issues, several organizations have sprung up. As an example, organizations such as the FCNA, which is part of ISNA, have played a key role in addressing some of the interpretive challenges that come the way of Muslims practicing their faith in a non-Muslim country. There are several fatwas that have been issued by FCNA dealing with issues of business ethics as well as zakat and other financial matters.

Apart from contemporary examples such as the FCNA, we also have historical examples from societies such as India and Egypt, where religious commentaries on the Qur'an became sources of polemics and argumentation and helped shape ideas of nationalism, patriotism and the concept of a "community." As Zaman (2002) argues, the Qur'anic commentaries that were written by different scholars and religious leaders in the nineteenth century Indian subcontinent played a key role in this process. He gives us one example: "The author of the *I'la al-Sunan*, Zafar Ahmad Uthmani, was the nephew of Ashraf Ali Thanawi, who, as we saw, had played an active role in responding to the crisis precipitated by the incidence of apostasy in colonial India" (p. 42). Here, Uthmani's work on nationalism is quoted. Zaman argues that his commentary refuted the idea of a united nationalism based on racial or ethnic identity. Uthmani used prophetic traditions as well as arguments of his own to make a strong case for a separate homeland for Muslims – that is, Pakistan. To counter this, there were leaders like Mawlana Husayn Ahmad Madani, who used his own polemical style rooted in a more inclusive Deobandi school argument to refute this divisive ideology. Contrary to what is generally assumed, that tradition is an unchanging construct that is handed over from one generation to another and blindly imitated, this short example shows that tradition became part of an ongoing debate that shaped many of the discourses of nationalism among people of the subcontinent. While the context and challenges of the discourses of Islam and philanthropy are different in India than they are in the US, some analytical inferences can be drawn from these incidents.

Islamic philanthropy in the US has had what we would call a "public relations" struggle. While awareness of how Islamic ethical norms dictate Muslims' day-to-day life among the American public and policy makers is low, there is a growing desire among Muslim American organizations for their government to recognize the key importance of Islamic norms of giving. The various laws and ordinances that restrict charitable giving to certain organizations have had a "chilling effect" on charitable giving among Muslims according to an American Civil Liberties Union (ACLU) report that was released in 2009. The discourse of "war on terror" has had a deleterious effect on how Islamic philanthropy is viewed. Further, this has had an impact on how Muslim American organizations are creating discourses about philanthropy. We submit that these moves and discourses have made these organizations vigilant as well as wary about associating with international causes – especially those that question American power abroad. While social justice is a prime ethical requirement of Islamic giving, there seems to be a tension in how Muslim American organizations view their role in providing help to victims where their country is often seen as the aggressor.

With the NOI claiming to be a "Muslim" group and its incendiary rhetoric of race, the group positioned Islam in conflict with mainstream American norms and clearly in opposition to it. The challenge before groups such as ISNA was largely to counter this negative stereotyping of Muslims and Islam in the US (Haddad and Harb, 2014). As we have seen, there are various ways in which Islam in America has been conceptualized: as an "indigenous" religion by groups such as the NOI and as a "foreign" faith by others. While cultural pluralists have sought to lessen the dissonance between these two competing narratives, some groups in the American political space have sought to portray Islam in America as an "other" (Haddad and Harb, 2014).

From a Foucaldian perspective, the entire discourse of Islamic philanthropy gives some people the power to rationalize and decide which forms of philanthropy are "legitimate" or not. Further, this occurs as a "whole group of relations is involved" (Foucault, 1972, p. 53). In the case of Islamic philanthropy, these relations are between the *Ulama*, government, the common man and nonprofit organizations. This discursive formation is evident in today's manner of administration of philanthropy by Muslim American nonprofits as well as the governance functions that it has to perform at both local and global levels. While we have not fully developed our argument of how ISNA and the Black Muslims used reason as a discursive tool, we have provided some tentative examples and offered the analysis of two crises as instances of reason being used to justify actions (from a religious perspective), both of which involved fundraising, philanthropic values and so on. We would also go so far as to suggest that the very terms "Muslim American" and "Muslim American identity" are recent phenomena that could be seen as "discursive practices" in that these emerged in a certain context of racial, ethnic and other power relations.

CONCLUSION

We have attempted, in this short chapter, to show that Islamic philanthropy is being interpreted as a "discursive tradition" in the US by leaders of Muslim organizations, who are thus providing new interpretive models, while working in various traditional systems that have been codified and set as benchmarks by classical Islamic scholars. These models offer new ways of making sense of zakat and sadaqa, which go beyond the traditional ways of understanding these practices and offer avenues – such as humanitarian aid and community development – for the practice of zakat and sadaqa. Discourses of giving around specific crisis events, we have argued, give us clues about how this process occurs.

The central mediating factor seems to be "reason" and the reinterpretation of religious tradition. While traditionally there has been a tension between how much to interpret the norms of Islamic philanthropy and how much to follow "as is," there has been a constant refrain from accommodation when it comes to interpretive practices in normative Islam. While practicing Muslims follow traditional norms in giving, there seems to be a growing awareness and acceptance of the use of reasoning and a pragmatic awareness of the need for reimagining the norms of zakat in America. While not exhaustive, the discussion in this chapter has touched upon some salient points that can be developed further.

Using two crisis situations – the First Gulf War of 1990 and the attacks of September 11, 2001 – we have also argued that the framing of Islamic philanthropy among Muslims in America by Muslim leaders has been carried out in a pragmatic, yet "traditional" manner, thus making sure that while traditional practices are respected, there is an awareness of the need for "innovation" in this sector. While the organizational discourses from the Muslim NGOs have clashed or not resonated with other institutional or governmental discourses, there has often been a recourse to accommodation, innovation in methodologies or, at times, radical rethinking of the ethical norms in Islam, that would justify a certain course of action. The discourse of social justice has been a recurring one in Islamic philanthropy and one that both the groups under examination – ISNA and the Black Muslims – have adopted, in varying degrees, to justify their work and gain legitimacy.

By using the discourses of community development, Muslim cosmopolitanism and ethnic ties, both organizations and leaders have gained legitimacy among the grassroots American communities and channeled religious giving towards causes such as education and community development. As Haddad and Harb argue, "American Muslims are increasingly choosing to integrate into American society through participation in and production of American culture in both civil engagement and in new, innovative ways such as political involvement, scholarship and interfaith engagement" (2014, p. 478). While there are a tiny minority of Muslims who are very rigid in their interpretation of how they view their theology, most major Muslim American organizations – both religious and nonreligious – are open to collaborating, incorporating and working with those with whom they do not necessarily share the same theological/epistemic lens when it comes to religious issues. As Siddiqui (2014) argues, "Due to their incredible diversity, Muslim Americans are largely cultural pluralists. They draw from each other and our national culture to develop their religious identity and values. Religious identity does not remain constant or uniform. Instead it is shaped by the interactions between the diverse groups that comprise Muslim America" (p. 215). This interaction that Siddiqui points to is key to the development of the Muslim American identity, which is taking shape, slowly. In the competing and at times conflicting discourses of how Islam should be practiced, Muslim American organizations are not only contributing to the debate on the role of religion in America, but also defining their own place in the American social fabric. This debate may further our understanding of how religion, religious authority and the power to shape discourses in the public sphere occurs in contemporary America.

While the American government's efforts at regulating and managing the fall out of the militant NOI were seen as a necessity by many, the current surveillance of Muslims by the New York Police Department (NYPD) and other measures to curb the civil liberties of Muslim nonprofit groups are seen as violating the basic rights of Muslim Americans

(Haddad and Harb, 2014). One can see in these measures a conflation of various discourses with that of philanthropy. These include discourses of national security, identity, poverty and international affairs.

It is interesting to note that the two groups under examination in this article – the Black Muslims and ISNA – responded very differently to similar situations, and their internal dynamics of power were also quite distinct. While we have shown that the Black Muslims sought global legitimacy from the Muslim world, ISNA sought local legitimacy through alliances with the American government as well as local interfaith groups. Their respective discourses have also been towards establishing this dialogue with groups that have been instrumental in helping them survive and remain meaningful. Pragmatism seems to be the guiding force for most American groups in terms of reconciling their beliefs with the realities that face them. While this does not imply that they are compromising on their traditional beliefs, one must recall that Islamic norms allow for a vast range of interpretive strategies for these groups to find their path in a complex and interconnected world. This fact has allowed for a healthy "discursive tradition" in the field of Islamic philanthropy to exist. The organizations in question are doing well and their missions remain relevant. All the while, their educational agendas – of being sources of learning, knowledge and organization and the mediators for creating an "authentic American Islam" – have remained central to their missions.

NOTES

1. See http://www.blackpast.org/1964-malcolm-x-s-speech-founding-rally-organization-af ro-american-unity.
2. See "The Crisis of Knowledge," available at https://www.youtube.com/watch?v=NIc-4CdIF9U (accessed February 2017).
3. See "For American Muslims, Everything Did Not Change after 9/11," available at http://religionandpolitics.org/2012/07/05/for-american-muslims-everything-did-not-change-after-911/ (accessed February 2017).
4. "For American Muslims, Everything Did Not Change after 9/11."
5. See "Text: Obama's Speech in Cairo," available at http://www.nytimes.com/2009/06/04/us/politics/04obama.text.html (accessed July 2017).
6. "For American Muslims, Everything Did Not Change after 9/11."

REFERENCES

Alterman, J.B. and K. von Hippel (eds.) (2007), *Understanding Islamic Charities*. Washington, DC: Center for Strategic and International Studies.
Asad, T. (1986), *The Idea of an Anthropology of Islam*. Washington, DC: Center for Contemporary Arab Studies.

Bekkers, R. and P. Weipking (2011), "A Literature Review of the Empirical Studies of Philanthropy: Eight Mechanisms that Drive Charitable Giving," *Nonprofit and Voluntary Sector Quarterly*, 40 (5), 924–973.

Benthall, J. (2008), *Returning to Religion*. London: I.B. Tauris.

Benthall, J. and J. Bellion-Jourdan (2003), *The Charitable Crescent: Politics of Aid in the Muslim World*. London: I.B. Tauris.

Boin, A., P. t' Hart, E. Stern and B. Sundelius (2005), *Public Leadership under Pressure*. Cambridge: Cambridge University Press.

Brooks, A. (2005), "Does Social Capital Make You More Generous?" *Social Science Quarterly*, 86 (1), 1–15.

Davidson, J.D. and R.E. Pyle (1994), "Passing the Plate in Affluent Churches: Why Some Members Give More than Others," *Review of Religious Research*, 36 (2), 181–200.

Ernst, C. (2003), *Following Muhammad: Rethinking Islam in the Contemporary World*. Chapel Hill, NC: University of North Carolina Press.

Esposito, J. and I. Kalin (2011), *Islamophobia: The Challenges of Pluralism in the 21st Century*. New York: Oxford University Press.

Foucault, M. (1972), *The Archaeology of Knowledge: And the Discourse on Language*. New York: Pantheon Books.

Frumkin, P. (2006), *Strategic Giving: The Art and Science of Philanthropy*. Chicago: University of Chicago Press.

Gee, J.P. (2011), *How to Do Discourse Analysis*. New York: Routledge.

GhaneaBassiri, K. (2010). *A History of Islam in America: From the New World to the New World Order*. Cambridge: Cambridge University Press.

Giving USA (2013), *Giving USA: Annual Report on Philanthropy*. Indianapolis and Philadelphia: Giving USA.

Haddad, Y.Y. and N.N. Harb (2014), "Post-9/11: Making Islam an American Religion," *Religions*, 5 (2), 477–501.

Hermann, M.G, C.F. Hermann and J.D. Hagan (1987), "How Decision Units Shape Foreign Policy Behavior," in C.F. Hermann, C.W. Kegley, Jr. and J.N. Rosenau (eds.), *New Directions in the Study of Foreign Policy*. London: Allen & Unwin.

Hudson Institute (2012), *The Index of Global Philanthropy and Remittances, 2012*.

Jackson, S. (2008), *Islam and the BlackAmerican: Looking toward the Third Insurrection*. New York: Oxford University Press.

Jamal, Z. (2011), *Ten Years after 9/11*. Washington, DC: ISPU.

Leaman, O. (1985), *An Introduction to Classical Islamic Philosophy*. Cambridge: Cambridge University Press.

MacIntyre, A. (1977), "Epistemological Crises, Dramatic Narrative and the Philosophy of Science," *The Monist*, 60 (4), 453–472.

Marx, J.D. (2000), "Women and Human Services Giving," *Social Work*, 45 (1), 27–38.

Ramadhan, T. (2001), *Islam, the West and the Challenges of Modernity*. Leicester, UK: The Islamic Foundation.

Safi, O. (2003), *Progressive Muslims: On Justice, Gender and Pluralism*. Oxford: Oneworld Publications.

Schervish, P. and J. Havens (2002), "The Boston Area Diary Study and the Moral Citizenship of Care," *Voluntas: International Journal of Voluntary and Nonprofit Organizations*, 13 (1), 47–71.

Siddiqui, S. (2014), *Navigating Identity through Philanthropy: A History of the Islamic Society of North America (1979–2008)*. PhD Dissertation, Indiana University.

Singer, A. (2008), *Charity in Islamic Societies*. Cambridge: Cambridge University Press.

Zaman, M. (2002), *The Ulama in Contemporary Islam*. Princeton, NJ: Princeton University Press.

3. Muslim philanthropy and nonprofit institutions in America

Muslim presence in America has been a matter of considerable dispute. While those who seek to see their current presence as a "foreign invasion" would suggest that this is a post-World War II phenomenon, Muslim Americans counter that Muslims have been present in America since before Christopher Columbus (GhaneaBassiri, 2010, p. 1). Some scholars argue that going as far back as nearly two centuries before Christopher Columbus arrived in America, Muslims sailed back and forth to America. Some even argue that Muslims were part of the crew of Christopher Columbus (Smith, 1999, p. 50). We do not have enough evidence to corroborate this argument, although the ascendance of Ferdinand and Isabella to the throne of Spain, the conquest of Islamic Grenada and the expulsion of Muslims could have led many to hop onto ships headed to the New World. In fact, by the late 1500s Muslim sounding names (such as Hassan, Osman, Amar, Ali and Ramadan) started appearing in official colonial documents (Curtis, 2009, p. 5). There is considerably more evidence of forced migration of West African Muslims as part of the slave trade (GhaneaBassiri, 2010, p. 15). Rich biographies of slaves confirm the presence of Muslims brought to America in this fashion. A recent Public Broadcasting Service (PBS) documentary, *Prince Amongst Slaves*, traces the history of a West African Muslim prince captured and sold into slavery.

At the founding of the United States, Thomas Jefferson is reported to have consulted the Muslim religious book, the Qur'an. Denise Spellberg, in her 2013 book *Thomas Jefferson's Qur'an: Islam and the Founders*, discusses Islam and its role in the early debates regarding a secular state and the place of Islam in American society (p. 3). At the 1788 North Carolina Convention to ratify the proposed US Constitution, William Lancaster, a staunch Anti-Federalist, explained what would happen in the future, when a Muslim would be elected to serve as president of the United States: "This is most certain . . . Mohometans may take it. I see nothing against it" (Hammer and Safi, 2013, p. 1). Mahometans was the term used for Muslims at the time. Subsequent to the forced migration of Muslim slaves from West Africa, America has seen five waves of Muslim immigration to the US starting from 1975 to the current day (Smith, 1999, p. 51–52).

Despite this long presence of Muslims in America, Islam failed to survive the first generation of its arrival until the twentieth century. There have been different reasons for the faith not surviving the generation. These include, but are not limited to, slaves not being permitted to practice their faith and the inhuman practice of breaking up slave families through sale; fierce anti-Islamic sentiment in the US; the fact that many of the migrations only included men coming for work or employment.

We argue that the lack of Muslim nonprofit institutions, like mosques and schools, until the twentieth century prevented the preservation and promulgation of the faith beyond the first generation. Religion has been the responsibility of the nonprofit and private sector due to the US Constitution's separation of church and state. The growth of Muslims in America and the similar growth of the US nonprofit sector has been instrumental in the development of Muslim American nonprofit organizations. While the history of this sector has been documented in other studies, our focus in this chapter is the development and growth of Islamic schools in America.

In 2008, a few hundred years after the North Carolina constitutional convention, Senator Obama's presidential campaign was dogged by a false narrative that he was actually Muslim. Colin Powell was critical of Senator McCain who failed to respond to this narrative from people supporting his candidacy:

> What if [Obama] is [a Muslim]? Is there something wrong with being a Muslim in this country? The answer is: No, that's not America. Is there something wrong with some seven-year-old Muslim-American kid believing he or she can be president? Yet I have heard senior members of my own party drop the suggestion: he's a Muslim, and he might be associated with terrorists. This is not the way we should be doing it in America.[1]

We also argue that Islamophobia has been at the heart of the development of Muslim identity, philanthropy and nonprofit institutional development. From the Spanish Inquisition and slaves not being permitted to practice their faith to immigration policies that targeted non-Europeans and Muslims there has been a long history of documented Islamophobia throughout the US's history. Kambiz GhaneaBassiri provides us with a historical analysis of this troubled past in *A History of Islam in America.* Carl Ernst's edited volume, *Islamophobia in America: The Anatomy of Intolerance*, unpacks this long history of Islamophobia.

Understanding the evolution and development of nonprofit organizations, and particularly Islamic schools, would be incomplete without an examination of Islamophobia and its long history in America.

ISLAMOPHOBIA

By Islamophobia, we mean the tropes and narratives that paint Islam as the "other." These tropes borrow from Orientalist imaginings of Muslims as uncivilized "others" and Westerners as the bearers of civilization. Liz Jackson argues, "Islam has rarely been discussed in this [American education] context. Similarly, Warren Nord's comprehensive . . . volume titled *Religion and American Education* has but a handful of sentences discussing Islam and Muslims" (Jackson, 2014, p. 1). According to Jackson, despite religion becoming recognized as an issue within American education in 1980s, it isn't until after September 11, 2001 that we see major research on this subject. Knowledge of Muslims and Islam within the education context in particular, and the American public in general, has been skewed by the media's depiction of 23 percent of the world's population. According to the Council on American–Islamic Relations (CAIR, 2006), 25 percent of Americans believe that Islam is a religion of hate, 10 percent believe that Muslims worship the moon god, 80 percent of those polled had never heard from a Muslim denouncing terrorism and 63 percent stated that their information came from television.

But to think that Islamophobia is a new phenomenon would be to undermine the history of bigotry in the US. According to GhaneaBassiri,

> Islam was generally associated with licentiousness and despotism under the Ottoman Empire, which was a waning but nonetheless formidable rival of Western European states in the eighteenth and nineteenth centuries. Thomas Bluett thus wrote about Job [a known Muslim slave at the time]: "tis known he was *Mahometan*, but more moderate in his Sentiments than most of that Religion are." (2010, p. 27)

When Prince Abdul Rahman was discovered in slavery and was brought to the North to raise funds to purchase the freedom of his children who remained in slavery, he was presented as a convert to Christianity (GhaneaBassiri, 2010, p. 28).

Alexander Russell Webb's mission to propagate Islam in America met with similar perceptual challenges of Islam. As GhaneaBassiri describes:

> Prejudices against Islam also ran so deep that even Theosophists, who counted among the free-thinking truth-seekers . . . were highly skeptical and disapproved of Webb's mission. One of the founding presidents of the Theosophical Society . . . who was one of the more sympathetic . . . towards Webb's mission, nonetheless described Islam "as that iron body of bigoted intolerance . . ." (p. 124)

Even Inayat Khan, who was sent to the US to propagate Islam, did not explicitly promote Islam. In fact initiates were not required to convert to Islam (GhaneaBassiri, 2010, p. 129). Khan writes about the prejudice against Islam in America:

> The prejudice against Islam that exists in the West was another difficulty for me. Many think Sufism to be a mystical side of Islam, and the thought was supported by the encyclopedias, which speak of Sufism as having sprung from Islam, and they were confirmed in this by knowing that I am Moslem [sic] by birth. Naturally I could not tell them that it is a Universal Message of the time, for every man is not ready to understand this. (GhaneaBassiri, 2010, p. 130)

It is of little surprise that Inayat Khan had to de-Islamize his teachings to gain legitimacy. We witness this even today, in popular American culture, where Rumi is the most read American poet but his work and life is often disassociated from Islam.

Senator Obama was not the first presidential candidate to face the ultimate slur of being a Muslim. Thomas Jefferson was attacked as being a secret Muslim for his argument that the US president should not have to meet a religious test (Spellberg, 2013, p. 9). Spellberg argues that, "by 1776 most American Protestants believed Islam to be the invention of Muhammad, of the prophet being a false prophet and an imposter. No matter their denomination, they had generally been primed not only from the pulpit but by books and theater to think the worst about Islam and Muslims" (2013, p. 14). This sentiment was framed in the popular understandings that many Westerners had of Islam, Spellberg points out. However, the founding fathers had a more positive view of Islam, by virtue of their reading and exchanges with Muslim countries. This fact alone may have helped guarantee equal protections for Islam as a religion worthy of recognition as an organized religion.

Carl Ernst argues that Islamophobia is a complex phenomenon in his important edited volume published in 2013 (Ernst, 2013, p. 2). He argues that we move from one extreme of thinking of Islam and Muslims as evil (Islamophobia) to the other extreme of seeing all Muslims as friends (Islamophilia). Muslims are a diverse group of individuals that cannot be essentialized into one narrative for the sake of perpetuating a specific point of view. Peter Gottschalk and Gabriel Greenberg argue that Islam and Muslims have always been put into an international frame so that they can be treated as "the other" (2013, p. 23). They argue that there are four broad dimensions of American fear of Muslims and Islam. First, there is anxiety about the social dimensions of Islam, perceptions that the faith is misogynistic, opposed to modernity and science and committed to sensual religion. Second, prejudices against foreign groups, in particular Arabs, are brought into this narrative by equating Islam with Arabs. Third, missionary Christian literature reinforces the inherent conflict between

Islam and Christianity. Finally, the Anglo-American heritage of the US brings forward prejudices from British colonial rule into our framework of analysis.

GhaneaBassiri, in the Ernst volume, argues that contemporary anti-Muslim bigotry must be analyzed within the broader history of religion and racial prejudice in America (GhaneaBassiri, 2013, p. 70). He argues that "bigotry and prejudice have played a central role in US history as a means of controlling racial and religious diversity and building national unity." Julianne Hammer, in the same volume, further deepens the dimension of Islamophobia by linking this narrative with gender. She states that the "gendered dimension of such discourses reveals the complex intersections of feminist, antiracist, and leftist, as well as liberal and neoconservative agendas . . ." (Hammer, 2013, p. 136).

Why is it important that we examine Islamophobia when analyzing Muslim American nonprofit institution building and in particular the development of Islamic schools? We argue that the context and environment within which a religious minority builds institutions to preserve and promote religious identity help determine the nature of that institution building. The physical environment determines whether builders dig basements or not; whether to build with brick, stone or wood; what colors should be used on the exterior and what materials we should use in the interior; and the foliage and plants that we select to accentuate the building. Similarly, the political and social environment determines the kinds of nonprofit institutions that are built (including the decision to build in the first place), especially when the builders perceive themselves and their identity to be under attack or scrutiny.

MUSLIM NONPROFIT ORGANIZATIONS IN AMERICA[2]

Muslim American nonprofit institution building has largely been focused on navigating religious identity through philanthropy. Muslim American charitable giving has been important in establishing religious institutions that further their faith, religious identity and place in American society. There are over 1200 mosques and 230 full-time Islamic schools in the US. Muslims have also used philanthropy to further the cause of social justice. Philanthropy has further been used by Muslim Americans to help create a unique Muslim American identity through the establishment of professional organizations, to fight for their civil rights by founding advocacy organizations and to give to Muslims living in developing countries through relief organizations. To connect Muslims with others relies on the power of association. Muslims have established numerous organizations in the US to support those who practice the Islam faith as well as to educate Muslims and non-Muslims alike in the tenets and values of Islam. Muslim Americans have historically founded many mutual-aid programs to further community goals.

As we have discussed earlier, the first large presence of Muslims in America resulted from the forced migration of Muslims from West Africa as slaves. While there is no evidence that Islam was able to survive slavery despite 10 percent of slaves being Muslims, there is evidence about how Islam affected African American tradition. Despite the lack of evidence of the development of Muslim American history, there is evidence that certain slaves sought to practice their faith, including almsgiving. Muslim slaves in Georgia are reported to have collected small quantities of rice every day from the rice paddies. They would also save small quantities of sugar from their rations. These Muslim Georgian women would then make a *saraka* cake. These cakes were given to children to eat. It is argued that the word saraka comes from the Arabic word *sadaqa*. Sadaqa is a form of Islamic philanthropy. Muslims who fail to give sadaqa are not committing a sin, but they are promised reward from God if they engage in this voluntary practice. There are no limitations on sadaqa, and it is presumed that most non-zakat charity by Muslims falls within this category. One can see how significant these cakes would have been in the difficult lives of the children of slaves. Not having money, the women did the only thing they could to continue to keep alive the charity that their faith asked of them. The situation that they were in influenced the nature of their philanthropy.

At the end of the nineteenth century, Alexander Russell Webb established the American Mission, also known as the American Islamic Propaganda and American Muslim Brotherhood, to further the cause of Islam in America (Abd-Allah, 2006, p. 159). Umar Abd-Allah documents the history of one of Islam's earliest and most high-profile converts in his book *A Muslim in Victorian America: The Life of Alexander Russell Webb*. Webb was the American consul to the Philippines when he converted to Islam. After traveling to India and connecting with the Islamic movement in that country, he returned to the US to spread the word about the faith. However, Webb's activities did not survive him, and no member of even his own family converted to Islam. His funeral was conducted at the Unitarian Church in 1916 in the presence of the local Muslim community (Abd-Allah, 2006, p. 267).

In 1910, a leader of the Sufi order came to the US to propagate Islam. He established the Sufi Order of America under the leadership of his earliest convert in San Francisco, Ada Martin (Curtis, 2010, p. 327). This order continued in different forms and was eventually reconstituted in the 1960s by his son.

While these instances of institution building are important milestones in history, they do not represent a cohesive and concerted effort to build Muslim American institutions. These organizations largely were dependent upon their founders. Most did not outlive their founders and none left an enduring footprint.

No serious institutional building by Muslims occurred until the twentieth century, the earliest organization being established by Noble Drew Ali in 1913 and named the Moorish Science Temple. This organization was predominantly an African American Muslim organization. Missionaries from India formed the Ahmadiyya movement in America in the 1920s. W.D. Fard and Elijah Muhammad established the Nation of Islam (NOI) in 1930, and this organization was also predominantly an African American Muslim organization. Lebanese immigrants established the Federation of Islamic Associations (FIA) in 1952 in the wake of Pan-Arabism that was promoted by Egypt's President Naser. In 1963, mainly Arabic speaking immigrant students formed the Muslim Student Association (MSA). This organization had both adherents of Jamaat-e-Islami of the subcontinent and the Muslim Brotherhood of the Middle East.

Mosques are important elements of the Muslim American philanthropic identity. The earliest mosque was established in 1925, but only 2 percent of modern mosques were established prior to 1950. The first still operating mosque in America was built in Cedar Rapids, Iowa in 1920 in a rented hall, with the mosque building being completed in 1934. However, in 1914 an Islamic center was established, which in 1924 became the Modern Age Arabian Islamic Society. In Ross, North Dakota, Muslims established a mosque in 1920 but had to later abandon it. The earliest mosque in New York was established in the 1930s by immigrants from Poland, Russia and Lithuania; the second mosque was also established in this decade, by a Moroccan immigrant, and was called the Islamic Mission of America. The earliest mosque in Michigan was established in 1919 in Dearborn, but had a very short lifespan. However, when the Ford Motor Company established a plant in Dearborn, the Arab Muslim community in Dearborn thrived, building a Sunni mosque in 1938 and a Shii mosque in 1940. Seven, primarily Lebanese, families who settled in the Boston area in the early 1900s worked towards the establishment of a mosque that was finally built in 1963.

Muslim Americans of World War II established the FIA in 1952 to fight for the right of Muslim American soldiers to have an "I" (designating Islamic faith) rather than "X" (designating unknown or nothing) on their military dog tags. The FIA is significant for a number of reasons. First, it indicates a larger community of Islamic organizations in the country that sought to "federate" or organize together. Second, this organization was established by second- and third-generation Muslim Americans who largely were war veterans. Finally, this organization pre-dated the final wave of Muslim immigrants to the US that would constitute the largest proportion of the current Muslim American population.

In 1971, Pakistani Americans with strong ties to Jamaat-e-Islami of Pakistan established the Islamic Circle of North America (ICNA). In 1982, major Muslim organizations including the MSA formed the Islamic Society of North America (ISNA). In 1992, mostly Arabic speaking leaders from the MSA and the ISNA established the Muslim American Society (MAS).

Since 1990 a number of public advocacy organizations have also been established, of which some major ones are the Council on American–Islamic Relations (CAIR, probably the largest with over 32 chapters), the Muslim Public Affairs Council (MPAC), the MAS Freedom Foundation and the American Muslim Alliance. This list does not include the many smaller regional or local public advocacy organizations that have been established by Muslims.

Every Muslim community is also home to multiple smaller nonprofits dedicated to causes dear to the founder. Nonprofits dealing with issues of domestic violence, scholarships for Muslims, feeding the poor, assisting the homeless, interfaith outreach, media and many others have been established across Muslim communities in the US.

In addition, nearly every college campus with a Muslim population has established an MSA, as have many high schools. Youth groups are popping up all over the country that encourage high-school and middle-school youth to be more involved with civic engagement as well as their faith. Muslim Americans are also part of larger civic organizations that they either join or "Muslimize." Muslim Boy and Girl Scout organizations are being established across the country. These smaller organizations take part in the Boy Scouts and Girl Scouts of America program, but the troops are all Muslim and run by Muslim parents. They incorporate Islamic events and programs into their activities.

Professional associations like the National Association of Muslim Lawyers, Islamic Medical Association of North America, American Muslim Social Scientists, Islamic Social Services Association, Association of Muslim Mental Health Professionals and American Muslim Scientists and Engineers are some further examples of organizations that have been established in the US.

Muslim nonprofits are not limited to the causes above and are as diverse as the Muslim population. A large proportion of Muslim Americans are immigrants with significant personal, familial and emotional ties to their home countries in the Muslim world. Furthermore, Muslims (both African American and immigrant) have emotional ties to the larger Muslim world as they see themselves as part of the larger Muslim Ummah (community). To support this element of their philanthropy they have established at least 12 major Muslim relief organizations in the US that raise money to be spent on relief projects primarily in the Muslim world.

Recent academic studies about Muslim Americans give us further understanding of philanthropy among Muslim Americans. The American Muslim Poll by the Zogby organization asked Muslim Americans if they were involved in various kinds of civic engagement (Zogby International, 2004). They defined "involved" as having donated time, money or having served as an officer of an organization. Of the Muslim Americans that were surveyed, 77 percent reported being involved with an organization to help the poor, sick, elderly or homeless; 71 percent reported being involved with a mosque or religious organization; 69 percent reported being involved with a school or youth program; 46 percent reported being involved in a professional organization; 45 percent reported being involved with a neighborhood, civic or community group; 42 percent reported being involved in an arts or cultural group; 36 percent reported being involved with an ethnic group; 33 percent reported being involved with a Muslim political or public affairs committee; 24 percent reported being involved with a veteran or military service organization; and 17 percent reported being involved with a trade or labor union.

The Pew Study reports that 76 percent of Muslim Americans reported that giving charity or zakat was very important, while an additional 14 percent stated that it was somewhat important; only 8 percent stated that it was not too important or not at all important (Pew Research Center, 2007). When ranking the five major religious practices, zakat was second only to fasting and came ahead of a pilgrimage to Mecca, reading the Qur'an daily and daily prayer. When combining "very important" with "somewhat important" it would be first.

Muslim American giving has been influenced by their religious and civic identity. Giving and volunteering is perceived as an important virtue in the US. It should be no surprise that Muslim Americans have sought religious values or ideas to further this American value. The US Constitution sepa-rates religion and state. Therefore, it should be no surprise that Muslim American religious institutions, like other American religious institutions, are largely within the nonprofit space. Furthermore, it should come as little surprise that the growth in Muslim American nonprofit institutions has occurred at an incredible rate, with growth being particularly strong in the 1960s, 1980s and since September 11, 2001 when we track similar growth in the US nonprofit sector. It is important to note that this nonprofit growth coincides with a growth in the Muslim American population. But it is similarly important to note the growth in the nonprofit sector in the US.

The growth of educational institutions to further religious education is not new to the American experience. Churches and synagogues (as well as other religious traditions) have long featured weekend or part-time religious education institutions to educate children and adults about faith. After-school clubs, such as the Fellowship of Christian Athletes, were developed to further religious education or promote bible study. More recently, we see children given time out of school so they can receive religious education at a local religious denomination of their choice. Over the past century, we have also seen the development of full-time religious schools that allow the integration of a state-mandated curriculum with religious education and values. Most notable of these is the Catholic school system in America. The focus of this book is the development of K-12 Islamic schools in America.

ISLAMIC SCHOOLS OF AMERICA

Educating Muslims about Islam has a long history. It was reported that the Prophet Muhammad would homeschool his daughter. His son-in-law and fourth caliph of Islam was similarly homeschooled. The history of education among Muslims around the world is a fascinating one that shows the various modes of cooperation and contestation of the institutions of higher learning with the state.

In the US, while there were attempts to educate or propagate Islam prior to the twentieth century (for example, Alexander Russell Webb's initiative), the current landscape draws its roots from the 1930s when the NOI established the University of Islam in Detroit. Malcolm X helps us to understand the need for such African American centered institutions. In his autobiography, he recounts how despite achieving excellent grades and seventh grade presidency, his teacher discouraged Malcolm from his dream of becoming an attorney and suggested that he become a carpenter (Haley, 1987, pp. 32–38). Within the vision of this public school teacher this was a trade better suited for an African American student. Racism and discrimination hindered the attainment of social movement through education. The NOI was committed to economic and social upliftment and these schools were an important aspect of that mission.

The NOI sought to make adult and child education a priority. But the need for children's education far outpaced adult education. By the 1970s there were nearly 40 schools within the Nation of Islam focused on K-12 education, largely situated in the inner city. These schools met two important needs in addition to the racism and discrimination being faced by African American Muslims: (1) religious education and (2) meeting the requirements of a population in light of a failing public school education in the inner city.

In the 1970s, upon the death of Elijah Muhammad, his Sunni Muslim son, W.D. Muhammad took over the NOI and the vast majority of the members converted to the Sunni tradition. The schools were rebranded as Sister Clara Muhammad Schools, named after the wife of Elijah Muhammad. These schools are largely situated in the inner cities and cater to a largely African American Muslim student audience. They are known for academic excellence and strong religious education. These schools remain an important part of the Muslim American K-12 schools landscape.

Not all members of the Nation of Islam were willing to convert to the Sunni tradition. A small minority, led by Louis Farrakhan, continued the mission of Nation of Islam. Under the leadership of Farrakhan, the University of Islam continued to serve the needs of his members. In the late 1990s, representatives from the University of Islam and Sister Clara Muhammad school system would send teachers to the ISNA Education Forum, which was largely attended by immigrant-established suburban schools.[3] These teachers eventually stopped taking advantage of the scholarship offered to both groups by ISNA, which covered conference fees and accommodations, because they felt that the needs of their institutions were not being addressed by training largely focused on teaching pedagogy and Islamization of the curriculum.

As we have discussed, the 1960s and 1970s resulted in a new significant wave of immigration of Muslims to America. By the 1980s these new immigrants were actively building institutions like Islamic centers and schools to meet the religious needs of the community and their families. These largely immigrant Muslim Americans sought to situate their families in homes in the suburbs. Suburbs offered security, good schools and a middle-class community. As these numbers grew, the demand for Islamic schools similarly also increased. As we will discuss in greater detail in Chapter 5, immigrant parents sought out full-time K-12 Islamic schools to shelter their children from social ills and to preserve Islamic cultural values, as well as to educate their children about Islam, allow them to receive training in the Arabic language and the Islamic holy book (the Qur'an), and enable them to achieve a high level of academic success, all of which public schools do not always provide.

This institution building resulted in the development of over 230 full-time Islamic schools in the US. These largely immigrant schools were the focus of our survey that we will discuss in greater detail in Chapter 5. Many Islamic schools started with the ideal of approaching mainstream curricula (like science, social studies, history and literature) through an Islamic perspective. However, Islamic schools today largely have the same texts used in public schools and have added Arabic, Qur'anic and Islamic studies to the curriculum. There is a growing trend for adding a character education component implemented through the curriculum. Fewer than 4 percent of Muslim American children attend these Islamic schools. However, these institutions have become an enduring and visible part of the Muslim American nonprofit landscape. They are more engaged in their communities in terms of activities than the Islamic centers, which largely only provide activities in the evenings and weekends. Islamic schools have employees, students and parents that can be more active within those institutions' missions. Islamic schools provide donors an opportunity to give towards educating young people about the faith domestically when there is heightened scrutiny and anxiety about giving overseas.

Islamic schools were an important priority for national organizations like the ISNA.[4] A majority of Islamic centers, mosques and Islamic schools in America today were built after ISNA's incorporation. It assisted in fundraising for those institutions by means of its speakers' bureau, constitution and by-laws; by extending ISNA's group tax exemption to local mosques (*masjids*); by issuing letters of support to overseas funders such as the Islamic Development Bank; and through its financial-service institution, the North American Islamic Trust (NAIT), which provided loans and investment opportunities and allowed communities to place their newly acquired centers in trust.

ISNA also developed an Islamic education curriculum, established two model full-time Islamic schools in Chicago and Toronto (Canada), and provided teacher and administrator training. The two full-time Islamic schools were an important achievement for ISNA. The Universal School in Chicago and the ISNA School in Toronto were models for other Muslim communities wanting to create private schools in suburbia. ISNA was again seeking to take an idea already rooted in North America, that is Sister Clara Muhammad Schools, and develop a model that it could disseminate. In its 1988 Annual Report, as cited in Siddiqui's dissertation, it not only announced the establishment of the new schools but also stressed the importance of an open and engaged process in achieving this milestone (Siddiqui, 2014). ISNA explained:

> How did they do it [establish an Islamic School]? From the beginning they made it very clear to people who was behind their effort. First they established a shura council for ISNA in Toronto, which has about a 100,000-strong Muslim

community. Then they organized the youth, the women, and the children under the umbrella of ISNA in order to inspire confidence in the community and gain credibility, a critical factor for anyone petitioning a community to entrust their children's education to them. Now open a school? Not yet. Next came an extensive survey of the community in 1982–83. . . . Finally, they recruited people who were truly leading figures in the community. In this way, parental trust was earned.[5]

ISNA's leadership wanted to urge its community to follow a course of building sustainable institutions. However, at the same time, they were concerned about external influences and worried that external funders could hijack grassroots institutions.[6]

The ISNA School in Toronto was established in 1984. An office was established in Chicago in 1983, but it took longer for this school to come into its own.[7] It was eventually established through the efforts of the local Muslim community with ISNA playing a supportive role. The school was officially established in 1990 and was named Universal School: The ISNA's Model Learning Center.[8] ISNA assisted in raising funds for this $2 million project by reaching out to local, national and international funders.

In addition to these model Islamic schools, ISNA's education department conducted extensive workshops for Muslim parents and teachers on establishing part-time Islamic education programs. Specifically, these workshops were designed to meet the need for educating Muslim children about Islam.[9] ISNA's leaders also sought to establish these part-time and full-time schools within an American context. For example, they publicly partnered with organizations like the National Council on Religion and Public Education (NCPRE).[10] Organizations like the NCPRE helped ISNA deliver effective programming, enhanced the organization's legitimacy and validated the organization's ability to serve in a national role.

The need for Islamic education and the growth of full-time K-12 Islamic schools resulted in the development of important national institutions being developed to serve this community. As mentioned, the ISNA provided considerable programmatic support and by 2000 had established the ISNA Education Forum. The Forum is the largest gathering of Islamic school principals, teachers and board members in the US. By 2016 they had started offering the main event in Chicago and a second event in California to meet with the geographic growth. Nearly 1000 educators from over 100 schools attend annually. The Islamic Schools League of America (ISLA) moderates an active LISTSERVE to support these educators. Their website offers critical learning tools for Islamic schools. ISLA also does research and surveys of these schools to provide us with important data.

A number of Sister Clara Muhammad Schools and immigrant schools came together under the auspices of ISNA to establish the Council of

Islamic Schools in North America (CISNA). CISNA holds its elections at the ISNA Education Forum, has a full-time executive director and in recent years has focused its efforts in assisting Islamic schools with issues related to accreditation.

Curriculum development has similarly been very important for this growing group of nonprofit organizations. The IQRA' International Education Foundation (Iqra), based in Chicago, was established to develop curricula, books and materials that are used by full-time and part-time Islamic schools. Iqra has developed K-12 materials for Islamic and Qur'anic studies that are used broadly. They also operate a large book store in Chicago. However, the diversity of the Muslim American community makes it difficult for any one institution to cater to the broad curricular needs focused on Islamic education. A number of other publishers have developed important books and materials that are used by Islamic schools.

In addition to traditional schools like the Sister Clara Muhammad Schools and other K-12 academic institutions there has also been the growth of traditional *madrasas* (colleges of Islamic Instruction) that are affiliated with the *Deoband* movement in India or *Tablighi Jamaat* movement of Pakistan. Many of these institutions are largely residential and focus mostly on religious education based on memorization of the Qur'an and Islamic knowledge. Students are encouraged to pursue a general equivalency diploma (GED) separately. These institutions are a very small part of the large Muslim American K-12 landscape.

Finally, Muslim Americans have also sought to shun formal education institutions and instead homeschool their children. Famous Muslim American leaders like Sheikh Hamza Yusuf have advocated in favor of this form of education and have embraced this for their own families. The focus of this book remains, however, on the K-12 formal institutions like the Sister Clara Muhammad Schools and suburban immigrant-established schools.

CONCLUSION

There has been a long history of Muslim presence in the US. However, despite that long history, Islam failed to survive the first generation until the twentieth century. The enduring presence of Muslim Americans today is due to the important institutions that were built in the twentieth and twenty-first centuries that provided an important vessel to develop religious identity in America. Due to the US Constitution's separation of church and state these institutions have largely existed in the nonprofit sector. The Muslim American nonprofit sector has grown dramatically following the new wave of immigration that started in the 1960s. Muslim American organizations saw rapid growth in the decades starting in the 1980s and this growth took on some urgency after the terrorist attacks on September 11, 2001. Islamic centers provided a place of worship and congregation, taking on religious, cultural and social responsibilities for the growing grassroots Muslim community. Advocacy organizations sought to fight stereotypes, hate crimes and discrimination, and relief organizations provided important vessels for paying alms. But the Muslim American nonprofit sector is incredibly diverse and embraces all aspects of the American nonprofit sector.

Islamic schools became an important vehicle to preserve and teach cultural, religious and social values for Muslim children. Like Catholic schools, they have developed into important communities of learning that further religious identity. While fewer than 4 percent of Muslim American children attend Islamic schools, these institutions have become visible anchors of the Muslim American community. Along with the Islamic center these schools represent important vehicles of community philanthropy and activity.

NOTES

1. See "Obama Endorsed by Colin Powell," available at http://www.washingtonpost.com/wp-dyn/content/article/2008/10/19/AR2008101900598_2.html?sid=ST2008101901990 (accessed July 27, 2017).
2. This section draws upon the previous work of co-author Shariq Siddiqui in three different chapters including Siddiqui (2013, 2010) and Curtis and Siddiqui (2010).
3. Co-author, Shariq Siddiqui, was a director at the ISNA and was responsible for the annual Education Forum.
4. This section related to ISNA and Islamic schools is taken from Siddiqui's dissertation (Siddiqui, 2014).
5. 1988 ISNA Annual Report, p. 20.
6. Interview with Dr. Sayyid M. Syeed, April 29 and 30, 2011.
7. ISNA Annual Report (1984) p. 5.
8. ISNA Annual Report (1989) p. 21.
9. ISNA Annual Report (1988) p. 19.
10. ISNA Annual Report (1988) p. 18.

REFERENCES

Abd-Allah, U.F. (2006), *A Muslim in Victorian America: The Life of Alexander Russell Webb.* New York: Oxford University Press.
CAIR (2006), *The Status of Muslim Civil Rights in the United States 2006: The Struggle for Equality.* Washington, DC: Council on American–Islamic Relations.
Curtis, E.E., IV (2009), *Muslims in America: A Short History.* New York: Oxford University Press.

Curtis, E.E., IV (ed.) (2010), *Encyclopedia of Muslim-American History* (Vol. 1 & 2). New York: Facts on File.

Curtis, E.E., IV and S. Siddiqui (2010), "Philanthropy," in E.E. Curtis IV (ed.), *Encyclopedia of Muslim-American History*. New York: Facts on File, pp. 449–452.

Ernst, C.W. (ed.), (2013), *Islamophobia in America: The Anatomy of Intolerance.* New York: Palgrave Macmillan.

GhaneaBassiri, K. (2010), *A History of Islam in America.* New York: Cambridge University Press.

GhaneaBassiri, K. (2013), "Islamophobia and American History: Religious Stereotyping and Out-Grouping of Muslims in the United States," in C.W. Ernst (ed.), *Islamophobia in America: The Anatomy of Intolerance.* New York: Palgrave Macmillan, pp. 53–74.

Gottschalk, P. and G. Greenberg (2013), "Common Heritage, Uncommon Fear: Islamophobia in the United States and British India, 1687–1947," in C.W. Ernst (ed.), *Islamophobia in America: The Anatomy of Intolerance.* New York: Palgrave Macmillan, pp. 21–52.

Haley, A. (1987), *The Autobiography of Malcolm X.* New York: Penguin Random House.

Hammer, J. (2013), "Center Stage: Gendered Islamophobia and Muslim Women," in C.W. Ernst (ed.), *Islamophobia in America: The Anatomy of Intolerance.* New York: Palgrave Macmillan, pp. 107–144.

Hammer, J. and O. Safi (eds.) (2013), *The Cambridge Companion to American Islam.* New York: Cambridge University Press.

Jackson, L. (2014), *Muslims and Islam in US Education: Reconsidering Multiculturalism.* New York: Routledge.

Pew Research Center (2007), *Muslim Americans: Middle Class and Mostly Mainstream.* Washington, DC: Pew Research Center.

Siddiqui, S.A. (2010), "Giving in the Way of God: Muslim Philanthropy in the United States," in D.H. Smith (ed.), *Religious Giving: For Love of God.* Bloomington, IN: Indiana University Press, pp. 28–48.

Siddiqui, S.A. (2013), "Myth vs. Reality: Muslim American Philanthropy since 9/11," in T.J. Davis (ed.), *Religion in Philanthropic Organizations: Family, Friend, Foe?* Bloomington, IN: Indiana University Press, pp. 213–214.

Siddiqui, S.A. (2014), *Navigating Identity through Philanthropy: A History of the Islamic Society of North America (1979–2008).* PhD Dissertation, Indiana University.

Smith, J.I. (1999), *Islam in America.* New York: Columbia University Press.

Spellberg, D.A. (2013), *Thomas Jefferson's Qur'an: Islam and the Founders.* New York: Random House.

Zogby International (2004), *Muslims in the American Public Square*, survey conducted by Zogby International for Georgetown University's Project MAPS, October 2004.

4. Identification and Muslim American philanthropy

The exercise of defining "Muslim Americans" is one of power. With no central religious or political authority defining who or what a "Muslim American" is, the definition of both "American" and "Muslim" has been variously interpreted and defined by various entities: the state, Muslim American groups, spiritual leaders and the media. There is often a conflation of meanings when people talk about a single "Muslim American" identity. By this, we mean a coming together of various ideas and identities – racial, ethnic, religious – that form this one single identity of a "Muslim American." For example, there is a debate pertaining to whether African Americans – who could be considered the original inheritors of the "Muslim American" identity, given their long history in the US – or the "immigrant" communities comprising Arabs, South Asians and others are the "real" Muslim Americans. Regardless, there seems to be a consensus that Muslims are an integral part of US culture and the religious landscape. This "identification" and growth of consciousness has both practical and theoretical implications in the realm of philanthropic giving.

This conflation of identities and communities and the resulting confusion has given rise to a discourse of "Muslim Americans" and "American Islam" which is often spoken about as if it were a unity. But as several scholars have pointed out (Jackson, 2008; Curtis, 2009; GhaneaBassiri, 2010), this idea of a "Muslim American identity" is an evolving idea and not a unified construct, as is often assumed. Where there is certainly a unity when it comes to agreeing on the "essentializing factors" (the so-called five pillars of Islam), this unity begins and, perhaps, ends there. This question of the emerging "Muslim American identity" is important, as it can help explain various sociological facts and also emerging phenomenon, including philanthropic behavior. As Muqtedar Khan, a scholar of American Islam, has argued, while in the early part of the twentieth century Muslim Americans were fighting to retain their "Muslimness" due to the cultural effects of living in a Western society, the Muslims of today seem to be fighting to retain their "Americanness" amid the climate of hostility and suspicion that their identity attracts (Khan, 2003). With the growing threats – both real and perceived – to religious tolerance in the US, this identity has become more pronounced, and several civil rights groups have emerged in the last few decades who are defining this "Muslim American" identity and how it should be perceived.

We make two related arguments in this chapter: (1) "Muslim American" identity is by nature plural, but has been appropriated by various groups, including the state apparatus, in an effort to "manage" the discourse related to Islam in the public domain; and (2) this "Muslim American" identity is a work in progress and can be seen as a negotiation between people and institutions in terms of relations of power.

This chapter is organized in four sections: In the first section we offer some demographic background of the Muslim American community and argue that there is no singular "community" but a plurality of "communities" that arguably make up the most diverse ethnic and racial group in the US. In the second section we offer some insights into the way that the state apparatus has tried to define what an "acceptable" Muslim American identity would look like. In the third section we outline the internal debates in the Muslim American community and look at how identity is shaped in America. Finally, in conclusion we offer some perspectives on how to fully conceptualize this category we call "Muslim American" as an organic one.

THE MUSLIM AMERICAN "COMMUNITIES"

There are about 3.5 million Muslims in the US. While the definite number of Muslim Americans is not known, because the US census does not collect data on religious affiliation, these estimates are cited by scholars and more widely claimed by Pew Research (GhaneaBassiri, 2010). Other estimates used by organizations such as the Council on American–Islamic Relations (CAIR) places this number between six to eight million. Amaney Jamal, a leading scholar of Arab American and Muslim communities, puts this figure at about ten million (Jamal, 2008).

The difficulty in defining the exact number of Muslim Americans is also compounded by the fact that there is no universally agreed-upon definition of a "Muslim" in America. This is because there is no central "Church" in Sunni Islam, which has a majority of the adherents of Islam (roughly 85 percent of all Muslims around the world are Sunni, while the rest are Shii or other smaller sects). While there is some religious authority in Shii Islam, it does not help address our problem. This ambiguity in who is a "Muslim" springs from the fact that many sects in the Muslim majority world fall outside of what is considered "Muslim" by "orthodox" Muslims. For instance, groups of Muslims such as Ahmadiyyas, who are followers of Mirza Ghulam Ahmed, a religious leader in pre-independence India, are considered heretical and, hence, outside the domain of "orthodox" Islam. However, in the US they would fall within the definition of mainstream Islam. The degree of plurality and diversity within Islam in the US is very high, though it is not well understood by those outside the faith community (Mottahedeh, 1987).

Similarly, Druze from the Middle East are also in a similar situation of being ambiguously defined as "Muslim." The situation is complicated when one considers some of the Muslim movements that have emerged in the US – for instance, in the case of Black American Islam, which had a lot of followers in the Nation of Islam (NOI), a movement started by Fard Muhammad in the early part of twentieth century (GhaneaBassiri, 2013). Fard Muhammad claimed to be God himself and propounded views that would clearly fit into the *Weltanschauung* (i.e. world view) of Islam as understood by those who read the Qur'an and believe in the finality of Prophet Muhammad's message. While the movement of the Historically Sunni African American Muslims (HSAAMs), which emerged out of the NOI to join "orthodox" Islam, has reduced this dissonance, it still remains. There are several non-orthodox beliefs among Black American Muslims and this becomes a point of contention for mainstream Muslims, many of who have a background or ancestry from South Asia or the Middle East (Siddiqui, 2014).

Added to this confusion is the division between Shii and Sunni Muslims and the different definitions of what is "authentic Islam." Many Sunnis take issue with the Shii beliefs in the role of Caliph Ali, and also their religious practices. Some extremely orthodox interpretations in Sunni Islam consider Shii as "non-Muslims." And finally, let us not forget the Sufis, the ecumenical "hippies" of Islam, who (in the contemporary era) seem to privilege "spirituality" rather than orthodox "practice" of religion. While Sufism in Asia is deeply connected with orthodoxy, in the West it manifests in a way that privileges "spirituality" over "orthodoxy." While religious orthodoxy cannot settle these disputes, as America is the most diverse Muslim American society there is, many Muslim American organizations (at least the national membership organizations) have come up with a pragmatic definition of who is a "Muslim." By their logic, anyone who proclaims or self-identifies as a Muslim is a Muslim.

Traditional Sunni methodology for choosing a "leader" or deciding on religious authority has relied on "*ijma*," or group consensus. This has been a preferred methodology for deciding which individual or group should lead a society. In an American context, marked by ethnic and racial diversity among Muslim Americans, there is the question of diversity of religious beliefs and what they take to be "Islamic" beliefs. Given this, we believe that a pragmatic understanding of Islam has emerged that seeks to accommodate differences rather than create boundaries and barriers to the practice of Islam among groups of people. This "pragmatism" has been alluded to by various religious leaders that we have interviewed for the purposes of this study.

Muslims are spread across the length and breadth of the US, but have a large presence in the metropolitan areas given that most jobs are located in and around big cities – New York has more than a million Muslims, as does the Washington DC area. There are a significant number of Muslims in California, Texas and Florida. The same goes for Chicago, which has a large South Asian and African Muslim American population. The American South does not have as many Muslims, but there are certainly a good number of Muslims in Virginia, Texas and other southern states.

As the Pew Research Center's report reminds us,

> Muslim Americans are a heavily immigrant population. Of those age 18 and older, more than six-in-ten (63%) were born abroad, and many are relative new-comers to the United States: Fully one-quarter of all U.S. Muslim adults (25%) have arrived in this country since 2000. The Muslim American population is also significantly younger and more racially diverse than the public as a whole. Muslim Americans are just as likely as other Americans to have a college degree, but fewer report having more than a high school education. (Pew Research Center, 2011, p. 13)

The report goes on to say that Pakistan is the largest country of origin for Muslim Americans, with 14 percent of first-generation immigrants, or about 9 percent of all Muslims in America, coming from there. Regionally, the Arab countries account for over 41 percent of all foreign-born Muslim Americans, while the rest are from sub-Saharan Africa, Europe and elsewhere. Racially too, there is immense diversity within the Muslim American communities. As the Pew report points out, "Muslim Americans are racially diverse. No single racial or ethnic group makes up more than 30% of the total. Overall, 30% describe themselves as white, 23 percent as Black, 21% as Asian, 6 percent as Hispanic and 19 percent as other or mixed race." With mixed-race marriages and greater ethnic mixing, this diversity is only increasing.

Given that there is no religious authority similar to the Catholic Church to adjudicate on these matters, the final word rests with the individual and the people involved. Authority is ultimately a sociological reality that is often negotiated through political, economic or other struggles. While Islamic tradition allows for reasoning within its parameters and defining what is "Islamic" and who is "Muslim," the reality of managing multiple identities is often difficult. It seems that Islamic tradition may perhaps help us answer this question. As Talal Asad argues in *Formations of the*

Secular, there is often a recourse to *ijtihad*, or reasoning, among "reformers" when they speak of "reforming Islam." He says that this is premised on universal rationality, which is not entirely needed when talking about Islam. The Islamic tradition provides "a theological vocabulary, a set of problems derived from the Qur'an and *Sunna* (the prophet's tradition) and major jurists, who have commented on both" (2003, p. 220). This means that though there are examples in the Islamic tradition to accommodate various schools of thought about who is "Muslim" or not, the definition in the American context seems to have been fluid and flexible, given the realities of American Islam being heavily influenced by Black American indigenous Islam and various other sects of Islam. As Sherman Jackson argues in *Islam and the Blackamerican* (2005), Black American Muslims have been influenced by Black folk religion and came to Islam through its influence. Islamic tradition, as we understand it, seems to have played a very small role in this process.

As one can see from the data above, Muslim Americans are diverse, not only in their origins, but also their beliefs. These disparate groups have formed several "communities" geographically, intellectually and spiritually. Mosques have played a key role in organizing community life, as both Siddiqui (2014) and GhaneaBassiri (2010) remind us. The mosques or Islamic centers have been places for people to gather, create communal lives, marry, conduct social events and so on, and have thus gone beyond the conventional role that is assigned to mosques in the rest of the world, where they are just places to pray.

Another way of organizing community has been through building institutions that serve Muslim Americans and the local communities. Organizations such as the Islamic Society of North America (ISNA), Council on American–Islamic Relations (CAIR) and the Muslim Public Affairs Council (MPAC) along with the National Association of Arab Americans (NAAA), Arab American Institute (AAI), Dearborn-based ACCESS and other national organizations that emerged in the 1990s have sought to help Muslim Americans participate in the political sphere, protect their rights and further the rights of Muslims around the world. Another set of organizations that have emerged are the humanitarian aid agencies. The most prominent of them are Islamic Relief and Helping Hand for Relief and Development, among others. These organizations can be seen as having created platforms for Muslim Americans to help organize and build a sense of community, both domestically and internationally.

Framing the Discussion of "Identity" Construction

There are several ways that identity can be understood in scholarship in sociology. Broadly speaking, there are three perspectives of identity in this field (Stets and Burke, 2000). The first perspective of identity is based on a group or collective beliefs, ideas and practices, as Stets and Burke point out. This could, for instance, involve occupational identity or religious identity. The second perspective of identity proposed by scholars such as Vaughan et al. (1981) and Wetherell and Potter (1988) considers identity to be embedded in a group or collective. The third perspective of identity is the social interactionist perspective, which analyzes the subjective meanings that people give to objects, events and behaviors. In this view, society is a social construction that occurs through human interpretation. Our analysis of the "Muslim American" identity will be through this third perspective.

To build our arguments, we will use Stuart Hall's (2000) notion of identity as a "process" that is not fixed. Hall's fundamental argument is that identity should not be seen as a "fixed" or permanent concept that is formed by a shared culture, heritage or ancestry. The second notion that he argues for is a framing of identity that is a work in progress. "If identity does not proceed, in a straight, unbroken line, from some fixed origin, how are we to understand its formation?" he asks; before answering his own question by saying that we must look for this identity formation through the ruptures and differences (Hall, 2000, p. 24). Hall examines these ruptures in the case of the Caribbean through factors such as slavery, colonization, forced labor and so on, whereas in the US they have evolved through slavery, trade and, more recently, immigration.

Stuart Hall (2000) reminds us that of late there has been an explosion in the discourse of identity and also an equal reaction to it in terms of criticism. This criticism has come from various perspectives, which seek to challenge the "notion of an integral, originary and unified identity" (p. 15). This sense of unified self, which is assumed to be present and continuous, is what is being criticized, Hall tells us. We find this idea directly relevant to discussion of a "unified Muslim American identity" that is being constructed by various intersecting discourses. One must note that this "unity" is an amalgam of various identities that are often at odds with one another (the Black American identity, the South Asian identity and the Arab identity), all jostling to find acceptance in the melting pot of America.

A similar call has been made by Alberto Melucci (1989), who says that in the social movements' literature there is a need for a "processual approach" to collective identity. His argument is also based on a constructivist view of collective action. Hall's call is to focus on developing a "theory of discursive practice" rather than developing a theory of the "knowing subject." By this, he means understanding how practices of identification among groups occur, rather than just focusing on the theoretical aspects of identity and its manifestation. The "identification" process is a construction, an ongoing negotiation between the agents involved. Hall acknowledges, similar to Melucci, that this process is an ongoing one that is never complete, in the case of Muslim American identity. But who decides in which direction this "identity" should move? What becomes a part of this identity and what gets left out? We suggest that this process is managed and controlled by various groups that represent the Muslim American identity. A close examination of how this process is unfolding tells us a lot about the power dynamics involved.

As Melucci argues, the term identity denotes the relationship between two actors that "allows their mutual recognition." His argument is that the notion of collective identity, which seems permanent, is in actuality an ongoing process. This means that the process involves continuous investments in organizational forms, systems of rules and leadership relationships (1989, p. 45). Where the self-reflective nature of group identity seems to face some resistance is in the recognition of this identity by others. In the case of Muslim Americans, this has been a dynamic process historically. For instance, with the NOI, a very racist (in the 1960s) and outwardly hateful group self-identified as "Muslim" and met with a lot of resistance both from mainstream American society and from other Sunni groups, domestically and internationally. It was only with the recognition of leaders such as Malcolm X by world leaders that Black American leadership and the NOI gained some recognition as authentic "Muslim" groups. The subsequent movement of NOI and its followers (at least the majority, if not all) to mainstream "Sunni" Islam brought the organization more legitimacy.

We are using the notion of identity in the sense that Stuart Hall does, that is, not in an essentialist manner, but rather in a "strategic and positional one." By this, we mean, following Hall, that this identity is not just a semantic signifier, but an unfolding one that is shaped by forces that are both internal and external to the individual and group. This definition of identity acknowledges that identities are never fixed or unified, but rather fragmented and fractured and constructed over "multiple levels of intersecting and antagonistic discourses, practices and positions" (Hall, 2000, p. 17). We will explore how this translates into practice in the next section.

Conceptualizing Muslim Americans as a Religious Group

The history of Muslim Americans can be seen as either a series of waves of immigration or one of an emerging "new" religious group. While scholars in the past have seen Muslim Americans as "immigrants" who came here and established their traditions, a recent wave of scholarship has emerged that seeks to study Muslim Americans (and Western Muslims in general) and locate them in "relation" to the mainstream of their societies. Reed College professor Kambiz GhaneaBassiri could be considered the leading proponent of this school of thought, and he suggests that Islamic traditions and values have developed in relation to the dominant ideas and traditions around them, and that a process of exchange and dialogue has occurred, which is often not acknowledged in existing scholarship on Islam in America (GhaneaBassiri, 2010). On the other hand, there is also a move to "religify" this group of people we call "Muslim Americans." While the narrative of Muslim Americans was written with ethnicity as the primary focus, it is increasingly being written with religion as the front-and-center issue. This "religification" of identity is an interesting phenomenon (Ghaffar-Kucher, 2009). It comes with its own sets of challenges, both for scholars and for practitioners.

GhaneaBassiri further argues that the dichotomy of American Islam and the "West" is a false one and that this is not how history has been shaped. This false binary reeks of Orientalist assumptions that dominated the thinking of eighteenth-century Europeans in their views on modernity and Islam. "In sum, determining whether or not a modern Islam or an American Islamic identity exists has been a stepping stone towards assessing the degree of conflict we may expect between a 'modern west' and a 'Muslim orient,' between American society and the Muslims within it" (GhaneaBassiri, 2010, p. 5). These discourses of the "East" and "West" that GhaneaBassiri points to are playing out even today. Whether it is the "Muslim ban" on travel by the Trump administration or the legislation banning the Muslim Brotherhood that has been introduced by Senator Ted Cruz, these discourses continue to impinge on the Muslim American community-building efforts.

While there is no agreed-upon definition of what "modern Islam" looks like, nor what an "American Islamic identity" should include, the consensus among community members seems to suggest that there is a growing trend for defining what this identity should look like. His observation is worth examining closely, considering that there have been various ways in which Muslim Americans have made sense of their own lives and identities in their adopted country. This has ranged from adopting some non-Muslim practices – such as celebration of Thanksgiving and Christmas

– to finding common ground in others. The range of improvisational practices has been quite impressive, argues GhaneaBassiri, pointing to the charitable practices of Muslims of Antebellum America, who preserved the charitable practices of their Muslim ancestors without knowing it.

Muqtedar Khan, a professor at the University of Delaware, argues that identity has two aspects: who we are and what we aspire to be. This entails a choice in terms of choosing what to reveal about oneself. Given that in a post-9/11 world, Muslims in America have been living under a microscope, with no privacy granted to them, the question of their identity has also become salient, he argues. "Everything that is visible and invisible is politicized. We don't know if the manifestation of identity is going to be enduring or not," he adds.[1] Khan argues that while in the 1970s the focus was on protecting the "Muslimness" of Muslim Americans, the focus more recently has been to protect the "Americanness," meaning that there is a greater political activism rather than purely identity politics.

Similarly, in his essay "Constructing the American Muslim Identity," Muqtedar Khan argues that the very forces that are shaping American society at large are also shaping the Muslim American community (Khan, 2003). Multiculturalism, growing activism among the Muslim elite and, finally, Islamic resurgence are three factors he outlines as being responsible for the increased salience of Muslim American identity in the US.[2] To this, we would add a fourth element, that is, the greater self-awareness and self-conscious attitude of young Muslim Americans. Young, educated Muslim Americans seem to be a part of this important identity creation mix, as youth groups such as Muslim Student Associations (MSAs) are increasingly asserting their right to their identity in the public sphere.

GhaneaBassiri further argues that Muslim immigrants arrived in the nineteenth century to find a national ideal that was still very much white and Protestant. And as their numbers grew, they would continue to be branded as foreign and a threat to the government of the US. Eventually, Jews and Catholics would win acceptance, but Muslims would be the "last to struggle for inclusion from among the founding triad of non-Protestant outsiders" (GhaneaBassiri, 2010, p. 274). This struggle continues, and was exacerbated immediately following the attacks on September 11, 2001. The passage of the PATRIOT Act undid a lot of civil liberties for Americans and put the spotlight on Muslims. This was also the turning point for the formation of a new "Muslim American" identity. As GhaneaBassiri argues, the manner in which Muslim Americans are making sense of their own "Muslimness" is through improvisational practices, accommodation and, in some cases, incorporating elements of mainstream culture into their religious practices – celebrating *iftars*, or the end of fasting meal during Ramadhan, with non-Muslims, for example.

Improvisational Practices and the Muslim American Identity

Another example of this strategy is the discourse of "interfaith" relations that seems to have become an important development in the formation of a "Muslim American" identity. "This is a very recent development, one that is about twenty years old or so. When I was getting my PhD, inter-faith was an alien word," said Dr. William Enright, former director of the Lake Institute on Faith & Giving.[3] This seems to be echoed in many of the interviews we conducted, including with Imam Hendi, Muslim chap-lain at Georgetown University, who pointed out that Jews, Muslims and Christians could be seen as part of the "*Ummah*," or a nominal brother-hood in Islam. This seems to be a phenomenon that is gaining traction. Indeed, there are several examples of such interfaith collaboration. For instance, the Friday *Juma'ah* is held at the Episcopal Church in downtown Washington DC, since there is no mosque in the area. Speaking of the inter-faith work that Islamic Relief does, Anwar Khan, CEO of Islamic Relief USA, pointed out that they sometimes gather material/tools and donate to Salvation Army. "Through inter-faith work, we are not only raising money, but also building bonds of love," he pointed out.[4] While interfaith work is being seen as a way to bridge gaps between various religious groups, in some contexts it has also come under criticism. An example is that of the Shalom Hartman Institute's program on Jewish–Muslim dialogue. As the program is fully sponsored by the Shalom Hartman Institute, and involves taking a group of Muslim leaders to Israel on a paid program, it has come under severe criticism for not showcasing the Palestinian side of the narra-tive, and it has been called "faith-washing" for its alleged ignoring of the political dimensions of the activity (Bazian, 2015).

Is it likely that Muslim Americans are appropriating aspects of "Civil Religion" to find space in the public imagination for their identity? Civil Religion, in the sense that Bellah argues for, is "an institutionalized collec-tion of sacred beliefs about the American nation" (Bellah, 1967). Bellah has argued that most Americans share the civil religious beliefs, symbols and rituals that "provide a religious dimension to the entirety of American life." It seems that the manner in which American Islam is evolving is also an indication of how Muslim American groups are in some cases incorpo-rating and tapping into this "Civil Religion" while choosing the narrative of American exceptionalism.

This way of interpreting and practicing "Islamic values" of cooperation is also found in conceptions of *maslaha* (welfare) and *darura* (necessity) that often face communities. Talal Asad points out that this "change of tradition" is argued on the basis of the aforementioned concepts in Islamic tradition (Asad, 2003, p. 221). Indeed, in Islamic history there are many examples of the Prophet Muhammad praying in a church and allowing Christians to pray in a mosque. The flexible and "open" interpretation of what is "Islamically" permissible seems to be rooted in such traditions of Islamic praxis. This is also tied to the radical "individualism" prevalent in American society, a phenomenon well explored by scholars such as Robert Putnam (2001) and Robert Bellah (1969), among others. Reza Aslan argues that this individualism is quite visible among Muslim Americans, both individually and collectively, as seen in the ways that Muslims in the US embrace their identity and flaunt it.[5]

THE "ADMINISTRATIVE STATE" AND THE EMERGENCE OF A MUSLIM AMERICAN IDENTITY

"Administrative state" is a term coined by Dwight Waldo and is the title of the dissertation that he wrote at Yale and which later became a book (Waldo, 1948). In it he argues that the function of government bureaucracies should be public service, not efficient running or "scientific management" of services. This gives rise to a natural tension between democracy and bureaucracy. While the assumption today is that public administration as a function is purely "scientific," Waldo argued that it involves an element of political theory and "values" of creating a democratic and just society (Waldo, 1948). We suggest that a closer examination of the administrative norms of the state can help us understand how the "Muslim American" identity is evolving as it pertains to public interactions with the state apparatus and civic discourse about Islam.

The increasing dominance of business thinking on public administration and the working of the government is a unique phenomenon, one that has gone in the reverse direction argues Waldo. This is evident when we see important decisions such as the Supreme Court ruling in the *Citizens United vs. FEC* case, which effectively gave unlimited powers to corporate entities to dominate the world of politics through campaign financing.[6] While the ideal of the "Great Society" was for bureaucrats to "manage" or create conditions for good business to flourish, the opposite has happened in the US. The ensuing impact has been a drive towards "greater efficiency" in government functioning and a greater focus on outsourcing – from social service provision to research to many other functions of the government (Cnaan and Dilulio, 2002). The "New Public Management" movement in public administration has had a profound impact on how social groups have been conceptualized and managed (du Gay, 1996). Du Gay makes the argument that the values that permeate this way of thinking are antithetical to those of "service" and a democratic way of governing.

Ever since the Great Society programs were rolled out, there has been tension between the government bureaucracy and community-based organizations and non-governmental organizations (NGOs). This tension has also played out and continues to play out in Muslim American communities, as they struggle to define how close or distant they would be with whichever administration was in charge.

Consider this: On October 22, 2011, President Obama addressed a gathering of Muslim American leaders and said:

> Here at the White House, we have a tradition of hosting *iftars* that goes back several years, just as we host Christmas parties and Seders and Diwali celebrations. And these events celebrate the role of faith in the lives of the American people. They remind us of the basic truth that we are all children of God, and we all draw strength and a sense of purpose from our beliefs. These events are also an affirmation of who we are as Americans.[7]

This act of communal sharing of food and participating in building a "community" through celebrating the act of breaking fast is symbolic. GhaneaBassiri argues in his essay "Religious Normativity and Praxis among American Muslims" that such adaptive practices have helped merge individual Muslims' relationship with the state with individual Muslims' relationship with the larger Muslim community and thus helped establish a "distinct American Islam" (GhaneaBassiri, 2013, p. 225). While not without controversy, these measures have sought to create not just an identity, but also a space for the government to "negotiate" its terms of engagement with the chosen leaders of the community.

Similarly, in an *iftar* hosted in 2014, President Obama used the occasion to honor a member of the Ahmadiyaa community, address the ongoing tension in Gaza at that time and also the role of Egypt in acting as a mediating force for peace. These occasions can be seen as events that are not just opportunities to find out whether one has "arrived" in Washington DC circles, but also chances to ascertain whether one's work as a Muslim group in the US has been legitimized by the state apparatus. For example, some prominent groups such as CAIR, one of the most prominent human rights and advocacy groups, are not invited to these *iftars* and gatherings, as they have taken a critical position in the past and also continue to question many of the domestic and international policies of the US administration. While they enjoy enormous legitimacy within the Muslim American community (most activists and Muslim leaders acknowledge that CAIR is the most popular Muslim American group), they continue to be shunned by the state apparatus.

These *iftar* dinners and engagement of Muslim American groups and individuals with the state apparatus has caused a lot of internal debate. The debate concerns whether these groups are doing a disservice to "Islam" and "Muslims" in the US and abroad by buying into the discourse of national security and not "questioning" the state and holding the president up to higher standards of ethical behavior. This debate becomes vociferous and has led in the recent past to a variety of acrimonious exchanges on social media, articles in Islamic magazines and online journals about whether this constitutes a lack of integrity on the part of Muslim groups who are self-professed defenders of human rights and dignity. Islamic traditions do place a lot of emphasis on social justice, equality and fighting against oppression. The criticism of these initiatives is that by not questioning the established discourse on matters that impact Muslims around the world, these Muslims who engage with the state apparatus are groveling to those in power. A similar debate played out when the All Dulles Areas Muslim Society (ADAMS) president, Imam Magid, participated in the prayer service during President Donald Trump's inauguration.[8]

We contend that by looking at the practices of the "administrative state" one can learn a lot about not only how civil religion is being shaped in America, but also how Muslim American identity is being molded. We argue that this is occurring in a dialectical relationship based on various forces – both domestic and international. The "religification" of Muslim American identity, as Ameena Ghaffar-Kucher has called it, is a phenomenon that has been written about (Ghaffar-Kucher, 2009). By this, she means an over-emphasis on the religious identity of an individual or community, at the risk of ignoring the other identities involved. We build on this and offer a perspective on how this is occurring in the corridors of power and on the American street.

PHILANTHROPY, IDENTITY AND MUSLIM AMERICAN COMMUNITIES

As mentioned at the beginning of this chapter, mosque building, as well as forming other "community" based organizations, has been crucial to the formation of a Muslim American identity. This process has occurred through philanthropic giving among Muslims. A lot of support has, in the past, come from wealthy donors from around the world. In the last two decades, there has been a growing recognition that "local" money should be invested in building mosques and other institutions, and one can point to the strong local support towards building these institutions as evidenced by data from several interviews.[9]

Let us examine how the discourse of Muslim American identity has evolved over the past few decades. Siddiqui argues in *Navigating Identity through Philanthropy* (2014) that ISNA accepted the idea of a "single Muslim identity," one that was culturally plural, but it came at a price. He traces the history of ISNA from its establishment in 1979 (officially in 1981) and places it within the context of the contestation and negotiation that took place between the HSAAMs, who were former member of the NOI, the cultural pluralists (younger members who sought to reconcile with American democracy, values of pluralism, etc.) and the "activists," who were strongly affiliated with international movements such as the Muslim brotherhood or Jamaat-e-Islami in the Indian subcontinent. In the struggle for power among these three groups, Siddiqui suggests that, ultimately, the cultural pluralist narrative won, and that the national recognition of ISNA as the "model" of Muslim Americans demonstrates this fact.

As a background to this development, one must note that the negotiation and bargaining with one's identity began much earlier than the 1980s, as GhaneaBassiri suggests. While the early Muslims, the slaves who were brought to the US in the seventeenth and eighteenth century, could not preserve their authentic religion, those who came in the twentieth century – as free men and women – could do so, and they sought to establish community organizations and groups that would preserve their religion and way of life.

Between the two World Wars, Muslim Americans started to "settle" permanently and to found their own institutions, argues Kambiz GhaneaBassiri in his book *A History of Islam in America* (2010). While the early pioneers, who came to the US in the first part of the twentieth century, sought to gain material wealth and send it back home, the interwar years changed this thinking and many started to consider America as their new home, he argues. GhaneaBassiri says that the new immigrants saw that the white Protestants claimed this country as theirs by virtue of a "conflation of race, religion and progress," and hence there followed Muslims, from Asia, Eastern Europe, Levant and Anatolia who began to claim America as their own on the basis of their prosperity.

GhaneaBassiri makes a very important point about their integration into America. He claims that often we tend to see their story through the lens of assimilation, but their actions suggest otherwise. "They did not assimilate into someone else's America, but rather were negotiating their own understanding of the relationship of Islam and America through the establishment of mosques and Muslim organizations and their political activities" (GhaneaBassiri, 2010, p. 171). This sense of "belonging" to America, both as an imaginary homeland and as a refuge from persecution (which it was for many, including refugees from the Levant, the Muslim brotherhood loyalists who fled political persecution in Egypt and Indian Nationalists who came in the aftermath of India's independence), also meant that they felt compelled to create the kind of home they wanted to live in. This "salad bowl" model of immigration that the US allows for has helped Muslim Americans retain some aspects of the culture from their countries of origin while adapting to the new country. With the African American Muslims, the challenge is one of negotiating their relationship with the "new" immigrant communities and finding their voice when it comes to representing the great umbrella of Muslim American communities.

As regards the evolution of the pacifist, establishment-oriented, pluralistic identity that "Muslim Americans" have adopted, Siddiqui argues that "ISNA's story is that of a newly established Muslim American identity, one that both 'establishment' Muslim Americans and the United States government embraced." The latter's support came after September 11, 2001, when American national security interests required a Muslim American identity that could be a mediating force with Muslim Americans and the Muslim world. America's acceptance of ISNA as the single Muslim American identity over others came at a heavy price – racial, ethnic and ideological segregation. Siddiqui places the emergence of this identity in the context of discourses of national security – the need for an American Islam that could be palatable to the entire American establishment (unlike the militant version of the NOI in the past), and could also mediate with the rest of the Muslim majority countries around the world.

Siddiqui includes "establishment Muslims," that is, Sunni Muslims, in his definition, but not Shiis and the NOI and other groups. Other scholars include the NOI; Edward Curtis and Sherman Jackson, two leading scholars of American Islam, take a more ecumenical approach to considering who is a "mainstream" Muslim. As the largest membership organization of its kind in the US, ISNA is a paradigmatic organization of sorts, which has carved a niche for itself in the country and "represents" Muslim Americans symbolically and tries to speak for them. Siddiqui argues that the presence of ISNA's then-president, Dr. Ingrid Mattson, at President Obama's inauguration signaled a level of acceptance of the organization – and, by proxy, of Muslim Americans – that had not occurred since Islam came to be recognized in the US.

Siddiqui's argument seems to go well with that made by Ghaffar-Kucher, whose study of Pakistani American youth in New York City suggests that there is an ongoing "religification" of their identity. By this she means that in the case of these Pakistani American youth, religion has emerged as the dominant identity both for them to identify with and for media and mainstream American society to "label" them with (Ghaffar-Kucher, 2009). Both Ghaffar-Kucher and Siddiqui seem to agree that this is an ongoing phenomenon in which the actors are actively involved in creating their identity in response to external events. While Ghaffar-Kucher places her analysis in the aftermath of September 11, 2001, Siddiqui goes back in history and starts his analysis with the Iranian Revolution, which he argues is the defining moment when Muslim American identity came to be defined. As Ghaffar-Kucher reminds us, religion is being increasingly used as a "marker of difference by mainstream in the U.S, and also the ethnic-religious groups themselves" (2009, p. 18). But the question that this brings up for us is: To what extent are the Muslim Americans themselves creating/constructing these differences "consciously," and in response to external forces? We will explore this question and related concerns in the next section.

The Six Forces Shaping Muslim American Identity

While the foregoing discussion has hinted at the external environmental forces, we have not yet outlined the combination of these external forces with internal drivers (that is, those within the community) for constructing a Muslim American identity. In this section we outline what we see to be a combination of forces, political and otherwise, that have influenced the development of a Muslim American identity (Figure 4.1).

While Figure 4.1 is heuristic and only indicative of what is possibly going on in the various Muslim communities, the reality is far more complex than represented in this figure. A brief discussion of internal and external forces follows, and we will outline how we see each as shaping the formation of Muslim American identity.

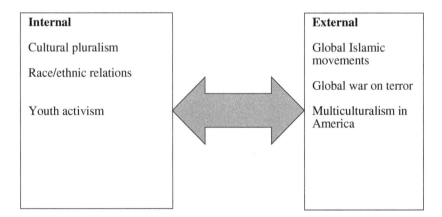

Figure 4.1 Forces shaping American Muslim identity

Internal forces

1. Cultural pluralism: As Siddiqui has argued, there has been an increasing trend in "mainstreaming" Islam among Muslim Americans (Siddiqui, 2014). This has meant that Muslim Americans have sought to make the public image of Islam acceptable and politically neutral. This has meant encouraging greater pluralism within the idea of what it means to be a "Muslim American." This trend is best exemplified in the strategic decisions made by ISNA to position itself as a mainstream American organization that is open to influences, ideas and positions from all directions – both within the community and from the government.
2. Race/ethnic relations: As several scholars have argued, the tensions between various ethnic groups in the US – the South Asians, Arabs and African-Americans – has shaped the identity formation of Muslim Americans. This continues to be one of the most important, yet understudied, aspects of American Islam.
3. Youth activism: As a predominantly young religious group, Muslim Americans are also witnessing youth activism in all areas of religious and public life; whether it is the call for greater gender inclusion in community decision making, the call for greater youth participation in mosque-level governance or international activism, the Muslim American youth are claiming greater right to participate in communal life. This is manifest through Muslim Students Associations on colleges campuses as well as through local activism at the grassroots level.

External forces

1. Global Islamic movements: Most scholars acknowledge that the early Islamic activists in the US were heavily influenced by activists from the Muslim Brotherhood, Jamat-e-Islami and other organizations (Jackson, 2005; Siddiqui, 2014). This influence continues, albeit to a smaller extent. While the priorities of these global Islamic movements are rooted in the context of the respective countries of their origin, the Muslim American groups seem to have accepted only parts of the solutions offered by these global Islamic movements towards building a "just" society where they can practice Islam.
2. Global war on terror: More than any other force, the global war on terror created a political rhetoric as well as policy changes that pitted "Good Muslim" against "Bad Muslim," as African academic Mahmud Mamdani has argued (Mamdani, 2004). This level of labeling and positioning of various "Islams" has arguably had a great impact not only on the growth of Islamic activism, but also on human

rights activism, with the proliferation of organizations such as CAIR, the Muslim Legal Fund and so on.

3. Multiculturalism in America: As one of the most multicultural and multiethnic nations in the world, the broader cultural impact on "American Islam" cannot be ignored. Whether it is operating in the realm of a capitalist framework, dealing with the challenge of maintaining an "Islamic ethical" framework in doing business, or getting educated, Muslim Americans are continuously faced with choices arising from living in a multicultural society. While "Islamic norms" by themselves are plural and encompass a global outlook, the particularities of operating in America make this choice quite daunting.

CONCLUSION

We have argued in this chapter that Muslim American identity is a social construct and that it has been variously shaped and formed by disparate forces including, but not limited to, the American state, Muslim American groups, individuals, the ruling elite and the media. Further, we have suggested that we must view the "Muslim American" identity as an ongoing negotiation, and not a static one that is formed and clearly defined.

Further to this, we have suggested that Muslim American practices offer us a glimpse into how this identity is being formed and shaped. GhaneaBassiri, in his essay "Writing Histories of Western Muslims" (2012), says that there are various approaches to understanding and framing the Muslim American experience. Whether the practices of Muslim Americans are to be understood through the lens of *Fiqh aqliyaat*, or the *fiqh* for Muslims in a "foreign" country, assuming that Islam in the US is but an expansion of global Islam, or whether we will understand Islam in America as a "native" or local religion and use categories of race, ethnicity and so on, is a matter of choice.

Others, such as Muqtedar Khan, another prominent scholar of American Islam, suggest that Muslim American exceptionalism should be seen from the perspective of many of the immigrants who value the freedoms that the US provides. He says,

> They hope that in America's society, where both freedom of religion and freedom of thought are protected, a genuinely authentic Islamic revivalist and reformist movement will emerge that will not only prove that Islamic principles are truly divine, but that will also establish a path for the Muslim community worldwide to negotiate the challenges of modernity. (Khan, 2012, p. 63)

His argument is that this "exceptional identity" is based on ideals of equality, fraternity, and freedom of speech and religion. But as we have seen earlier, this is an ideal that is often never realized in full. There are contestations and fights that take place to uphold these very ideals, and there is always a relation of power – a differential in power – that can make these realizations of equality and pluralism hard, if not impossible.

Finally, it is important to remember that identity and identity politics are always complicated matters that require nuance and perspective. To look at these issues in binaries of us versus them or in terms of set epistemologies is to miss the point entirely. GhaneaBassiri reminds us that Western Muslims, being both Islamic and Western, "occupy a conceptual space in modern discourses between these binary categories." This means that their lives challenge notions of "European indigeneity and Islamic authenticity." Further, he points out that "They also complicate the notion of diaspora because many of them are converts at home in their own lands, and others are third- and fourth-generation Western Muslims, who self-identify with no land other than where they were born and now live" (GhaneaBassiri, 2012, p. 172). This in-between space can help us re-examine our assumptions about Islam and Muslims. In particular, this unique situatedness of Muslim Americans can help us understand the way that America has evolved as a nation of sanctuary for persecuted populations and also how Muslims have come to evolve into their own community, with a distinct religious identity, in the US. Whether they are tenth-generation African Americans in Alabama or recent immigrants to Detroit, Muslim Americans are supposed to belong to a new category called "Muslim Americans."

As Melucci reminds us, the identity of collectives in cultural contexts should be seen as the product of conscious action and the "outcome of self-reflection more than a set of given or structural characteristics" (2000, p. 51). This means that the collective actor tends to construct itself within the limits of the environment and also within other social relations. Melucci suggests that we need to make a conceptual leap in terms of our understanding of identity in groups, and this is true in the case of Muslim Americans.

We have tried to problematize the "Muslim American identity" and looked at the vast diversity of debate regarding what it means to be a Muslim American, using examples of prominent discussions about leadership, moral vision for the community and so on. While these are specific instances of problems involving the "administrative state," questions of identity, citizenship, ethnicity and religion have become conflated, as they often are. How these bigger tensions will be ultimately resolved remains to be seen, as this is an ongoing negotiation between and among Muslim Americans.

NOTES

1. "Muslim American Identity with Muqtedar Khan," available at https://www.youtube.com/watch?v=hdzLFo0JTmE (accessed January 2017).
2. "Muslim American Identity with Muqtedar Khan."
3. Interview, June 2013.
4. Interview with Anwar Khan, October 2013.
5. "Dr. Aslan on the Future of the Middle East," available https://www.youtube.com/watch?v=KzhxSavDkP8 (accessed January 2017).
6. *Citizens United vs. Federal Election Commission*, available at http://www.scotusblog.com/case-files/cases/citizens-united-v-federal-election-commission/ (accessed January 2017).
7. "Text of Obama's Address at White House Iftar Dinner," available at https://blogs.wsj.com/washwire/2010/08/14/text-of-obamas-address-at-white-house-iftar-dinner/ (accessed January 2017).
8. "Washington-Area Imam Plans to Issue Muslim Call to Pray at Prayer Service," available at https://www.washingtonpost.com/local/2017/live-updates/politics/live-coverage-of-trumps-inauguration/washington-area-imam-plans-to-issue-muslim-call-to-pray-at-prayer-service/?utm_term=.34ff65b8bb99 (accessed January 2017).
9. Based on interviews for this specific project and those carried out by us between 2010 and 2016.

REFERENCES

Asad, T. (2003), *Formations of the Secular: Christianity, Islam, Modernism.* Stanford, CA: Stanford University Press.

Bazian, H. (2015), *Shalom Hartman's MLI Program: A Constructive Engagement.* Turkey Agenda.

Bellah, R. (1967), "Civil Religion in America," *Journal of the American Academy of Arts and Sciences*, Winter, 96 (1), 1–21 (in the issue titled *Religion in America*).

Bellah, R. (1969), "Religious Education," in R. Robertson (ed.), *The Sociology of Religion*. Baltimore, MD: Penguin Books, pp. 262–293.

Cnaan, R. and J. Dilulio (2002), *The Invisible Caring Hand: American Congregations and the Provision of Welfare*. New York: NYU Press.

Curtis, E.E., IV (2009), *Muslims in America: A Short History*. New York: Oxford University Press.

du Gay, P. (1996), "Organizing Identity: Entrepreneurial Governance and Public Management," in S. Hall and P. du Gay (eds.), *Questions of Cultural Identity*. Thousand Oaks, CA: Sage Publications, Inc.

Ghaffar-Kucher, A. (2009), "Citizenship and Belonging in an Age of Insecurity: Pakistani Immigrant Youth in New York City," in F. Vavrus and L. Bartlett (eds.), *Critical Approaches to Comparative Education: Vertical Case Studies from Africa, Europe, the Middle East, and the Americas*. New York: Palgrave Macmillan, pp. 163–178.

GhaneaBassiri, K. (2010), *A History of Islam in America: From the New World to the New World Order*. New York: Cambridge University Press.

GhaneaBassiri, K. (2012), "Writing Histories of Western Muslims," *Review of the Middle East Studies*, 46 (2), 170–179.

GhaneaBassiri, K. (2013), "Religious Normativity and Praxis among American

Muslims," in J. Hammer and O. Safi (eds.), *The Cambridge Companion to American Islam*. Cambridge: Cambridge University Press, pp. 208–227.

Hall, S. (2000), "Who Needs 'Identity'?" in P. du Gay, J. Evans and P. Redman (eds.), *Identity: A Reader*. Thousand Oaks, CA: Sage Publications, Inc., pp. 15–30.

Jackson, S. (2005), *Islam and the Blackamerican: Looking toward the Third Resurrection*. Oxford: Oxford University Press.

Jackson, W. (2008), *The Wisdom of Generosity: A Reader in American Philanthropy*. Texas: Baylor University Press.

Jamal, A. (2008), *Race and Arab Americans before and after 9/11: From Invisible Citizens to Visible Subjects*. Syracuse, NY: Syracuse University Press.

Khan, M.A.M. (2003), "Constructing the American Muslim Community," in Y.Y. Haddad, J.L. Smith and J.L. Esposito (eds.), *Religion and Immigration: Christian, Jewish and Muslim Experiences in the United States*. New York: Altamira Press. pp. 175–198.

Khan, M.A.M. (2012), "American Exceptionalism and American Muslims," *Review of Faith and International Affairs*, 10 (2), 56–65.

Mamdani, M. (2004), *Good Muslim, Bad Muslim: America, the Cold War, and the Roots of Terror*. New York: Pantheon Books.

Melucci, A. (1989), *Nomads of the Present: Social Movements and Individual Needs in Contemporary Society*. Edited by J. Keane and P. Mier. Philadelphia: Temple University Press.

Melucci, A. (2000), "The Process of Collective Identity," in K. Johnston and B. Klandermans (eds.), *Social Movements and Culture*. Minneapolis, MN: University of Minnesota Press, pp. 41–63.

Mottahedeh, R. (1987), *The Mantle of the Prophet: Religion and Politics in Iran*. Harmondsworth, UK: Penguin Books.

Pew Research Center (2011), *Muslim Americans: No Signs of Growth in Alienation or Support for Extremism*. Washington, DC: Pew Research Center.

Putnam, R.D. (2001), *Bowling Alone: The Collapse and Revival of American Community*. New York: Touchstone.

Siddiqui, S.A. (2014), *Navigating Identity through Philanthropy: A History of the Islamic Society of North America (1979–2008)*. PhD Dissertation, Indiana University.

Stets, J.E. and P.J. Burke (2000), "Identity Theory and Social Identity Theory," *Social Psychology Quarterly*, 63, 224–237.

Vaughan, G., H. Tajfel and J. Williams (1981), "Bias in Reward Allocation in an Intergroup and an Interpersonal Context," *Social Psychology Quarterly*, 44 (1), 37–42.

Waldo, D. (1948), *The Administrative State: A Study of the Political Theory of American Public Administration*. New York: The Roland Press Company.

Wetherell, M. and J. Potter (1988), "Discourse Analysis and the Identification of Interpretative Repertoires," in C. Antaki (ed.), *Analysing Everyday Explanation: A Casebook of Methods*. London: Sage Publications.

5. Philanthropy, institution building and legitimacy in Islamic schools in America

As we discussed in Chapter 3, there have been at least seven reported migrations of Muslims to the US since the fifteenth century. Despite this long interaction between Islam and the US, Islam was not able to survive past the first generation of Muslims until the twentieth century. The Civil Rights Movement, immigration laws and new tax laws coincided with a large migration of Muslims to the US after 1960 (GhaneaBassiri, 2010). Muslim Americans have sought to build places of worship, relief organizations and Islamic schools as a way of expressing their religious and philanthropic identity and of navigating modernity (Siddiqui, 2010). Muslim Americans have embraced the philanthropic sector as a way to mediate faith and practice.

This chapter presents the results of a national survey of full-time Islamic schools in the US and their governance practices during times of crisis (9/11 and Great Recession). There have been two prior attempts to collect national data from Islamic schools. The first was conducted by the Islamic Society of North America (ISNA) in 1989.[1] The second data collection was by the Islamic Schools League of America (ISLA) in 2004 (Keyworth, 2011). The survey results by the ISLA have been published in a number of academic arenas.

Our survey examines whether competition within the school district, greater bonding due to Islamophobia, and economic stress have influenced Islamic school governance practice. In addition, this chapter will provide demographic data regarding Islamic schools. We draw upon existing literature on competition, Islam in America, Muslim American philanthropy, nonprofit diversity and legitimacy to examine how Islamic schools continue to navigate the challenges of Islamophobia after September 11, 2001 followed by the economic challenges of the Great Recession of 2008. Our primary theoretical contribution is in re-examining the changing nature of philanthropy and its role in American Islamic schools. In particular, we examine how schools have navigated identity, public policy and performance in search of legitimacy.

RESEARCH QUESTIONS

We examine the following research questions through the results of our survey:

1.   How did 9/11 and subsequent policy changes in the US impact philanthropy, volunteerism and activities with respect to Islamic schools?
2.   How did the recession of 2008 impact philanthropy?
3.   What is the role of public policy in the schools' performance? Does it matter which school district these schools are located in?
4.   How do Islamic schools navigate and build their Islamic identity and gain legitimacy in the environment in which they operate?

In answering these questions, our goal is not only to show descriptively how these factors impact the workings of these schools, but also to develop from all this data a normative theory of effective community building, philanthropy and organizational identity.

Four main forces drive cultural and religious philanthropy among Muslim Americans, and these four forces are the organizing framework of the book. We also build on the ideas of philanthropy offered by contemporary scholars of philanthropy and Islam in America in order to see how our theories fit into the models proposed and to what extent our emerging theory is testable as being "strategic philanthropy."

First, there is *legitimacy*, which is among the key factors, and the drive to acquire both internal and external legitimacy in these schools. While the initial purpose for establishing Islamic schools was to preserve religion and culture, the felt need now seems to be towards providing an environment for maintaining values and norms among the newer generation of Muslim Americans. Islamic schools are asked to attain legitimacy internally by providing an "Islamic education," but must also provide a high-quality secular education that competes with the public school system. Without such legitimacy they would not attain sufficient enrollments or the philanthropic resources needed to sustain a nonprofit institution. These schools must also attain external legitimacy to ensure that, in a post-9/11 environment, they can withstand external scrutiny. Furthermore, in states with generous voucher programs, this external legitimacy brings about needed external resources. These external resources influence the importance of external legitimacy. The literature related to nonprofit legitimacy and neo-institutional theory is critical to this examination.

Second, we look at how many of the schools conceptualize and manage *Islamic identity*, and not necessarily as an inheritance from their parents or ancestors. While not fully assimilating with the mainstream society, these young men and women are expected to integrate, acculturate and practice Islamic values and norms, all the while becoming "model citizens" in America. This discursive move to incorporate tradition into education can be considered a discursive tradition, as the well-known anthropologist Talal Asad has suggested (Asad, 1986). The discourse of Islamic identity also relates to the idea of organizational identity and how these schools navigate this dimension while aiming to offer a quality education.

Third is *public policy*. We see a key role for both local and federal policy in not only regulating, but also allowing these schools to function unhindered. Although there have been some concerns about Islamic schools, both as institutions that promote "ghettoization" within the community and as institutions that promote narrow thinking, based on our research thus far, there is no legislation barring the functioning of these schools. We aim to incorporate the policy implications into our research and also find out to what extent both local governments and federal government policies can impact the growth and proliferation of these schools.

Fourth and finally is the role of *leadership*. While environmental factors are key to determining the sorts of challenges that present themselves to certain communities, leadership determines how these communities address those challenges. Although there is talk of a global "crisis of authority" in the Muslim world, we contend that this is not the case. At the local level, we see shining examples of remarkable leadership that have helped Muslim Americans not only to survive existential post-9/11 challenges, but also to thrive and build institutions – the very bedrock of any community. Thus, we examine the role of leadership in Islamic educational institutions.

Islamic schools, along with Islamic centers in the US, have become an important symbol of Muslim American institution building. Although Islamic schools educate less than 4 percent of Muslim American children, they have received both support and criticism. Internally, some Muslim Americans argue that Islamic schools create ghettos and take children away from a diverse American culture. Externally, some argue that Islamic schools are proponents of extremism. There is little definitive data to assert that either of these two assertions is accurate. However, this study along with previous studies of Islamic schools suggest that Islamic schools are taking needed steps in achieving legitimacy. While our study is ongoing, it is clear that Islamic schools have taken specific programmatic, governance and operational steps to attain legitimacy within the Muslim American community. Islamic schools confirm previous research suggesting that September 11, 2001 had no negative impact on their philanthropic resources and legitimacy. On the other hand, Islamic schools, like many American nonprofits, found the Great Recession challenging and saw a decline in their philanthropic resources.

ISLAMIC SCHOOLS

A large majority of the over 1200 Islamic centers and over 200 full-time Islamic schools were established after 1980. While these Islamic centers have been the focus of a few academic studies, Islamic schools remain relatively understudied in a post-9/11 context. This is despite the fact that Islamic schools remain some of the most stable and active philanthropic institutions in the Muslim American community (Haddad et al., 2009).

There are an estimated 235 full-time Islamic schools in the US (Keyworth, 2009). Islamic schools for the purpose of this chapter include full-time pre K-12 grade educational providers that incorporate an Islamic religious curriculum in addition to a traditional public school academic curriculum. Muslim parents send their children to Islamic schools for a number of reasons including instilling Islamic knowledge and values; providing second language instruction; sheltering from racial and religious discrimination resulting in bullying; and protecting children from social ills like drugs, alcohol, gang activity and sexual activity (Grewal and Coolidge, 2013, p. 246). Less than 4 percent of Muslim American youth attend full-time Islamic schools (Keyworth, 2009). However, the demand for Islamic schools is increasing (Grewal and Coolidge, 2013, p. 246).

Over 85 percent of all Islamic schools today were established in the 1990s by recent immigrants (primarily from the Middle East and South Asia). The majority of these schools are founded by Sunni Muslims, although they attract Shii children as well (Grewal and Coolidge, 2013, p. 250).

Islamic schools have come together and formed support organizations like the Council of Islamic Schools in North America (CISNA) and ISLA. These schools have resulted in the development of secondary support organizations that seek to provide Islamic curricula to help these schools fulfill the "Islamic" part of their identity. Muslim Americans have seen the rise of major nonprofit and for-profit corporations focused on providing Islamic, Qur'anic and Arabic studies curricula and materials, examples being Iqra Education Foundation, Sound Vision, Islamic Book Store and Noor Art.

Every year the ISNA organizes an annual Education Forum that hosts over 100 full-time Islamic schools and over 500 educators. This event provides educators with best practices and professional development through presentations from fellow educators (Siddiqui, 2014).

Islamic schools are becoming increasingly popular despite external attacks on these institutions (Grewal and Coolidge, 2013, p. 246). However, scholars have suggested that this popularity may be the result of a post-9/11 rise in philanthropy and support and therefore may be short-lived. This chapter examines the measures that Islamic schools are taking in establishing institutional legitimacy.

LEGITIMACY

Neo-institutional theory explores how nonprofit organizations seek to establish, build and maintain their legitimacy in the eyes of the public or the eyes of particular constituencies (Suchman, 1995, p. 571). The three types of legitimacy – pragmatic, moral and cognitive – are relevant for this study. Specifically, we can understand that Muslim American parents and communities see supporting Islamic schools as providing specific advantages to their families and community (pragmatic legitimacy). Due to heightened Islamophobia we see Islamic schools being adopted as anchor Muslim American institutions in addition to Islamic centers (moral legitimacy). Due to academic excellence, accreditation and other forms of educational legitimacy, Islamic schools have become a predictable feature of the Muslim American nonprofit sector (cognitive legitimacy).

The nonprofit sector is heavily institutionalized, where organizations have various, interdependent relationships. The essence of institutional theory is that organizational legitimacy depends not only on how the non-profit organization performs but also on how it is perceived. Therefore, organizational practices are influenced by what their leaders perceive as signals of legitimacy (Zucker, 1987, p. 443). However, this sociological framework is incomplete when we try to understand legitimacy within the nonprofit sector. Mark Suchman provides us with a helpfully more expansive review of the scholarship of institutional theories and organizational legitimacy (Suchman, 1995, p. 571).

To understand how Muslim American organizations have fought for and gained legitimacy, the ISNA serves as a "paradigmatic" case. As the most visible and influential organization in the US, ISNA functions as the convener, organizing force and moral voice of Muslim Americans. Given our familiarity with ISNA's work and its key role in the evolution of a Muslim American identity, we suggest that a brief discussion of its role is warranted before we delve into how Islamic schools have established their own legitimacy.

For the purpose of this chapter, we adopt the definition of legitimacy provided by Suchman: "Legitimacy is a generalized perception or assumption that the actions of an entity are desirable, proper, or appropriate within certain socially constructed systems of norms, values, beliefs, and definitions" (Suchman, 1995, p. 574). In a post-9/11 context, Muslim American organizations have struggled to establish legitimacy, both internally – within the communities – and externally, in the "mainstream." For instance, for the ISNA, legitimacy did not depend on specific events alone. Rather, its long-term legitimacy depended on a collection of events or history. Nevertheless, we will see that ISNA's legitimacy was at times influenced by singular events. Legitimacy does not always reflect reality. It is the perception of the organization or reputation of the organization. It is "possessed objectively, yet created subjectively" (Suchmann, 1995, p. 574).[2] Legitimacy is a social construct and can vary based on the audience. Any nonprofit organization, including ISNA, can be both legitimate and illegitimate, depending on the person or group making that judgment.

As we have stated, there are three broad types of legitimacy: pragmatic legitimacy, moral legitimacy and cognitive legitimacy (Suchman, 1995, p. 577). Pragmatic legitimacy is based on the self-interest of the organization's stakeholders. Support for ISNA depends on what value the constituent expects to receive from ISNA. This expectation can include direct personal benefit to the constituent. Alternatively, the constituent believes that ISNA furthers the constituent's overall beliefs. This support also stems from the belief that ISNA cares about the constituent.

Moral legitimacy depends on whether ISNA's actions are the right thing to do, rather than whether they merely benefit the audience. ISNA achieved moral legitimacy by operating in socially acceptable ways. ISNA's structure and the charisma of its organizational leaders also influence its moral legitimacy. Nonprofit organizations' claims to resources are based on the demonstration of their moral commitments (Ostrander and Schervish, 1990). Cognitive legitimacy is the most powerful form of legitimacy. ISNA attained cognitive legitimacy when people or institutions came to believe that ISNA is necessary or inevitable based on a taken-for-granted cultural framework (Suchman, 1995, p. 577).

Organizations can affect their legitimacy through their structure, mission statement, programs and outcomes (Oseewaarde et al., 2008, p. 42). Legitimacy can be a huge asset when an organization encounters short- or long-term declines in its organizational outcomes (Candler, 2001, p. 356). Religious organizations demonstrate a stronger ability to survive and retain legitimacy (Walker and McCarthy, 2010, p. 334). Jeavons suggests that religious organizations' behaviors are influenced by their commitment to integrity, concern for the public good and concern for the personal welfare of employees and volunteers (Jeavons, 1992, p. 410).

Integrity requires organizations like ISNA to be transparent and accountable. Religious organizations' concern for the public good is broader than just their immediate stakeholders and donors. Religious nonprofits seek to serve all within their faith and provide services to humanity at large. Finally, these organizations seek to treat those who help make the organizational work possible with genuine respect. ISNA, as a religious organization, relies upon both nonprofit and religious forms of legitimacy. Therefore, both Suchman's and Jeavons' frameworks are essential in understanding ISNA's quest for legitimacy.

LEGITIMACY IN SCHOOLS

Non-traditional schools make up a growing portion of the educational landscape (Paino et al., 2014, p. 501). Full-time Islamic schools have a similar burden to charter schools in trying to create a legitimate educational environment. Charter schools gain legitimacy when they are able to meet the educational needs of their communities and offer services in such a manner that they can attract students (Paino et al., 2014). Charter schools face attacks from public school proponents that harm their attainment of legitimacy (Vergari, 2007). Similarly, religious schools in America have also been seen as divisive and injurious to the missions of the public school (Perko, 2000). Key to legitimacy is the issue of accountability (Paino et al., 2014). The separation of church and state in the US requires minimal federal accountability of Islamic schools (Merry and Driessen, 2005). However, organizations like CISNA have been pushing for accreditation because this accreditation gives Islamic schools a seal of approval (Merry and Driessen, 2005). In fact, research suggests that despite a minimal amount of federal and state control, Islamic schools seek credibility (or legitimacy) by providing the children with an excellent education and interfacing with other schools and government officials to improve the education being offered (Merry and Driessen, 2005). American Islamic schools have embraced accountability in as many forms as are available to them through government and private means (Paino et al., 2014).

Accountability in private schools is governed by four factors (Figure 5.1):

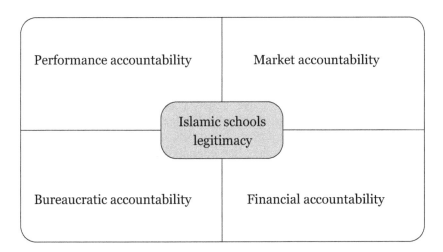

Figure 5.1 Legitimacy in non-traditional schools

performance, market, bureaucracy, and finance (Paino et al., 2014). Performance accountability is tied up with test scores and the academic success of the students. Market accountability depends upon the school's ability to meet the community's perceived needs. Bureaucratic account-ability depends upon following the laws and regulations that govern the school. Financial accountability involves the management of funding as well as transparency.

RESEARCH METHODS

This chapter presents the findings of a national survey of Islamic schools in the US. We initially identified a list of Islamic schools through the website of the ISLA. ISLA operates an active LISTSERVE, hosts an annual retreat of Islamic school administrators, performs data collection and provides best practices through its website (Keyworth, 2009). We found a list of 277 Islamic schools. The survey was then distributed in three ways. First, it was sent out to the ISLA LISTSERVE, second it was distributed at the 2014 Annual ISNA Education Forum held in Rosemont, Illinois, and finally it was mailed to the list. Thirty-seven proved to be wrong addresses. We received 1 returned with a note that the school declined to take part in the survey. Completed surveys were received from 45 schools.

The schools that responded were largely suburban and immigrant. We only received responses from two African American schools. Therefore, our findings are limited to Sunni, suburban and immigrant Islamic schools, though we had interviews with principals/board members of African American schools.

ANALYSIS

We carried out basic descriptive statistical analysis, looking for mean, median and averages across all variables. While the sample size was not suf-ficiently large for regression analysis, we believe these preliminary results offer us an initial window into the changing patterns of philanthropy among these communities. We believe that taken together with the qualita-tive findings, the results will form a rich empirical basis for us to analyze and draw conclusions.

RESULTS

The majority of schools (58 percent) were independent of the local Islamic centers, with their board being selected or elected by parents and donors. The majority of schools stated that their revenue largely came from tuition. Philanthropy was significant (over 20 percent) but played a minor role in the organizational budgets. Only 5 of the 45 respondent schools stated that they had a written strategic plan. The vast majority of the schools have a hybrid curriculum that includes state and religious curricula. Most schools reported that over 50 percent of their teachers were licensed. The vast majority of the schools reported that they were accredited. The majority of the respondents reported that their school did better academically than most of the schools in their district. The vast majority of schools reported that their student teacher ratio was 15:1 or less.

Most respondents indicated that their schools were suburban and middle class. Respondents stated that they relied upon philanthropy (donations, volunteers, grants) as the second most important source of revenue. Tuition represented the major source of funding for the respondent schools. Most schools reported that they received some sort of funding from government resources. This largely consisted of professional development and Title funding.

Most schools reported that "identity or brand" was important for their school. Only one school reported having non-Muslim students. Many schools reported that they were "very conscious of our Islamic identity." The majority of respondents reported no impact to their school or philanthropy as a result of 9/11. However, the majority of the respondents suggested that the 2008 recession impacted them negatively. This included reduction of donations or enrollment. However, the vast majority of respondents reported no decrease in volunteers as a result of the 2008 recession. An examination of internal and external legitimacy of Islamic schools in America provides us a context as to why these two events had differing consequences on these nonprofit organizations.

DISCUSSION

Islamic schools, like most Muslim nonprofits in the US, have faced two major crises in the past ten years. The first was the terrorist attacks on September 11, 2001. The second was the economic crisis in 2008 that led to the Great Recession. Islamic schools report differing perspectives about both events. September 11, 2001 marked a new era in American history. On the morning of that day, terrorists hijacked four airplanes, and while

Americans watched in horror, the terrorists crashed two of the planes into the Twin Towers in New York City.

At the time of these attacks, ISNA's outgoing president, Muzammil Siddiqi, was in Washington DC with leaders of various Muslim American organizations.[3] As part of the American Muslim Political Coordinating Council (AMPCC), they were in Washington to meet with the George W. Bush administration to raise concerns about the government's increasing hostility towards Islam and Muslims. Major Muslim American organizations had endorsed President Bush in his close election with Vice President Al Gore, and polls suggested that their vote had made a difference in states like Florida where the results had been close (Hanley, 2000). They felt that President Bush "owed them" for his victory and were seeking reaffirmation of assurances and promises made during the Bush campaign about his support on Muslim American issues. However, because of the terrorist attacks, this meeting never took place.

There was little immediate information about the terrorists on the morning of the attacks. However, Muslim American organizations immediately worked together and released a statement.[4] Within hours, national Muslim American leaders organized a united press release condemning the attacks and requesting quick apprehension of the perpetrators, while also urging restraint on the part of the media until the hijackers could be identified.[5] Much to the horror of Muslim Americans it was soon confirmed that the terrorists were Muslims from outside the US. The events of September 11, 2001 resulted in a new paradigm for Muslim Americans and their institutions. As GhaneaBassiri states, "9/11 tested the mettle of American Muslim institutions at both the local and national level. These institutions played a fundamental role in helping American Muslims weather the backlash of 9/11" (GhaneaBassiri, 2010, p. 362). Like the rest of the nation, Muslim Americans were afraid. Their fear was not from foreign terrorists but from the backlash of the American population.

Despite outreach to Muslim Americans by the US government, interfaith organizations and civil rights organizations, the instances of prejudice, Islamophobia and hate crimes continued to rise. It became politically expedient for some politicians to attack Muslim American organizations as extremists (Curtis, 2009, p. 100). Polling showed that many Americans viewed Muslims and Islam negatively. This tension between prejudice and acceptance of pluralism was not uniquely focused on Muslim Americans. It simply incorporated Muslim Americans into a deeper narrative of race relations and prejudice in America. Islamic centers and Muslim Americans reported an increase in hate crimes.

Islamic schools were at the forefront of these tensions. Islamic schools held classes five days a week and then offered their spaces to weekend schools. While Islamic centers or mosques may offer services five times a day, Islamic schools offered the greatest number of Muslim American targets for those who sought revenge. In addition, Islamic schools were not viewed from the prism of a religious school but as "madrasas" of terrorism. This was especially true as Americans learned that "Taliban" derived from the word "student."

Islamic schools in America were faced with two challenges. First internal legitimacy: Islamic schools, like all private schools, need students to exist. Second, Islamic schools needed external legitimacy to protect their institution and students. In exploring how Islamic schools sought legitimacy, Paino et al.'s four factors for accountability (performance, market, bureaucratic and financial) are useful for our analysis (Paino et al., 2014, p. 506).

Respondents to our survey suggest that Islamic schools took the necessary steps to achieve stronger academic performance from their students. When asked how their schools compare to other schools in their region, the respondents reported they did as well if not better, as we can see in Figure 5.2.[6]

If this assertion is true, it is important that we examine how Islamic schools were able to achieve academic success. An important factor for our analysis is the economic circumstances of the students and the geographic circumstances of the schools. When asked whether the schools were in urban or suburban districts the majority of schools reported that they were suburban schools as we can see in Figure 5.3.

Furthermore, when asked whether the school had predominantly

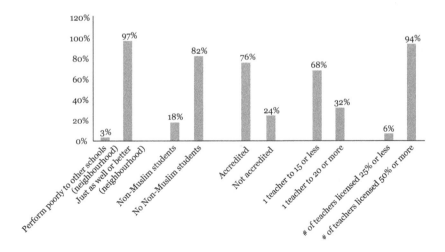

Figure 5.2   Performance accountability

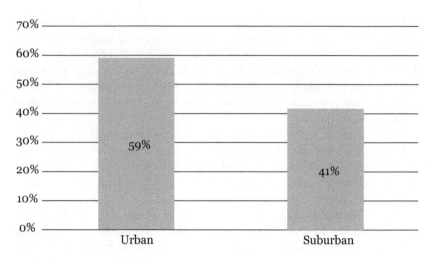

Figure 5.3   Geographic location

lower-income, middle-class or upper-class students, most respondents reported that they largely had middle-class students. Therefore, the urban and economic indicators help explain why the schools are "as good as other schools in the area." However, a number of respondents reported that their schools did better than schools in the area or in the state as we can see in Figure 5.2.

It is clear from the survey results that Islamic schools have taken active steps to ensure academic success. First, their selection of a hybrid curriculum ensures that the school children are afforded the same text-books, curricula and knowledge factors that help them to succeed in standardized tests.

Furthermore, Islamic schools have chosen to hire a large proportion of their teachers with teaching licenses and credentials. Many of these teach-ers are not necessarily Muslims. For example, one respondent school in Indiana has teachers for secular subjects that are all non-Muslim licensed teachers. They have Muslim faculty for Arabic, Qur'anic and Islamic studies only, due to the lack of Muslim licensed teachers in the state. Furthermore, while religious education is important, it represents less than 25 percent of the curriculum.

Finally, research suggests that student to teacher ratio has an impact on academic success (Mosteller, 1995, p. 113). Most respondents reported better student to teacher ratios than public schools.

However, it isn't just academic success that has led to the legitimacy of Islamic schools. Islamic schools have also sought market accountability.

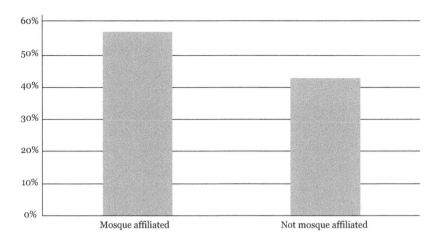

Figure 5.4a   Relationship with Islamic center

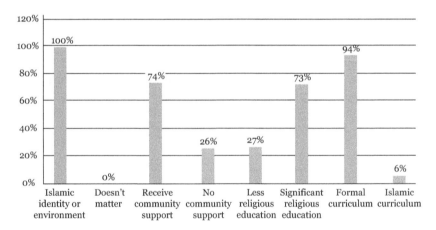

Figure 5.4b   Religious identity

Market accountability occurs when Islamic schools are able to identify and fulfill the needs of their community. Islamic schools' primary market for students are Muslim Americans living in their area. According to Grewal and Coolidge, Muslim parents send their children to Islamic schools for a number of reasons including instilling Islamic knowledge and values; providing second language instruction; sheltering from racial and religious discrimination resulting in bullying and protecting children from social ills like drugs, alcohol, gang activity and sexual activity (Grewal and Coolidge, 2013, p. 246).

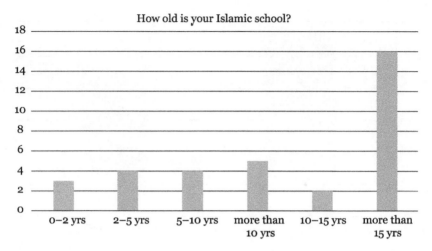

Figure 5.4c   Age of Islamic school

Islamic schools have responded to these concerns by signifying the importance of an Islamic identity. In our survey, an overwhelming number of Islamic schools stated that their Islamic identity was very important. They also reported that branding was very important for their school. Furthermore, most Islamic schools report that they are supported by the local Muslim community.

In addition, they have included a significant amount of religious education as we have seen in Figures 5.4a–c. See also Figures 5.5a and 5.5b.

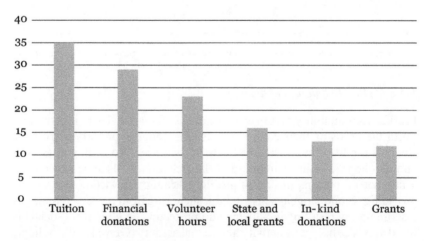

Figure 5.5a   Sources of revenue

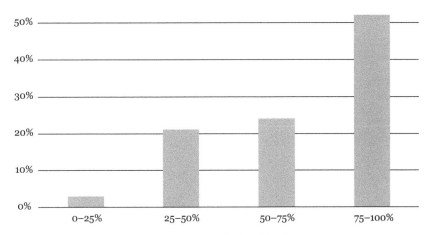

Figure 5.5b   Tuition as a proportion of school budget

Islamic schools have also sought to take steps in achieving bureaucratic accountability. Islamic schools largely report that they have sought and achieved accreditation (Figure 5.6).

Islamic schools have had mixed success in providing formalized reports and in receiving funding from state and local government (Figure 5.7).

Islamic schools report limited success in strategic planning.

Islamic schools have also had limited success in external legitimacy in terms of recruiting non-Muslim students despite their academic success.

Islamic schools have also taken important steps towards market account-

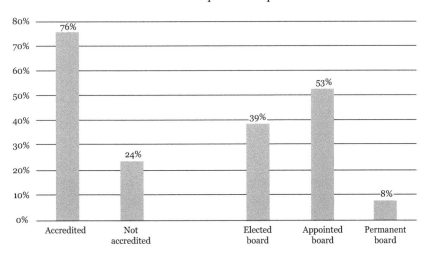

Figure 5.6   Accreditation/bureaucratic accountability

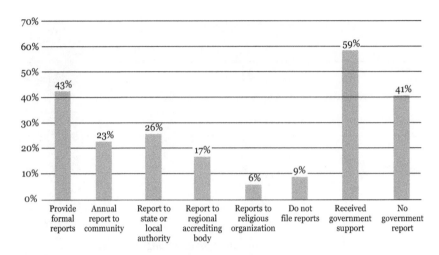

Figure 5.7   Financial accountability

ability. Islamic schools report that the main source of income for their schools is tuition (Figure 5.5a). See also Figure 5.8.

Islamic schools also seek out traditional sources of income for nonprofit organizations like donations, volunteer hours, grants and grants (Figure 5.5a). See also Figure 5.9.

However, Islamic schools report different results from the two crises they were asked about. Islamic schools generally saw no impact of the terrorist attacks of September 11, 2001 or saw an increase in philanthropy (Figure

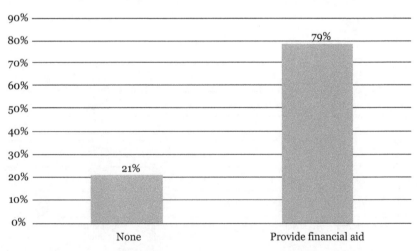

Figure 5.8   Financial aid

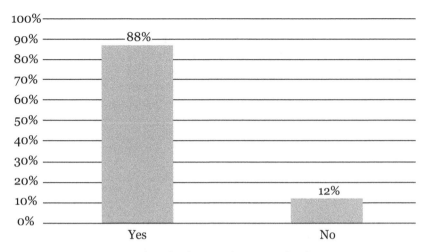

Figure 5.9 Do you conduct fundraisers for your school?

5.10). In fact, research from Grewal and Coolidge and from Siddiqui suggests that September 11, 2001 increased Muslim American institutional philanthropy and Islamic schools saw an increase in enrollment. Further, GhaneaBassiri suggests that crisis resulting in Islamophobia leads to a greater sense of Islamic identity and activism. Therefore, it is surprising that Islamic schools do not report a similar result.

It is likely that schools felt uncomfortable reporting a positive impact

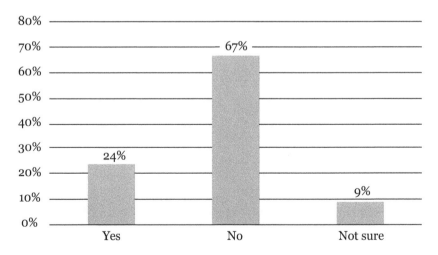

Figure 5.10 Did the scrutiny after September 11, 2001 impact your Islamic school?

of the terrorist attacks considering the Islamaphobic environment. Alternatively, it maybe that Islamic schools did not experience the growth that the Muslim American nonprofit sector did as a result of the heightened sense of Islamic identity and activism after 9/11.

The second crisis resulting from the Great Recession negatively impacted the American nonprofit sector. Islamic schools similarly report a negative

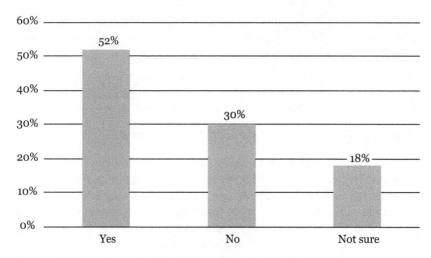

Figure 5.11   Did the 2008 recession impact school finances?

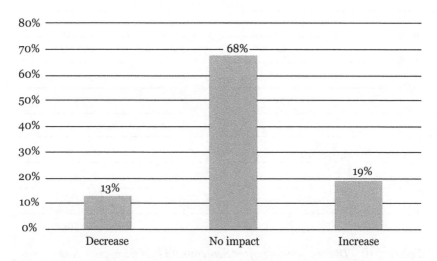

Figure 5.12   Impact of 2008 recession – volunteerism

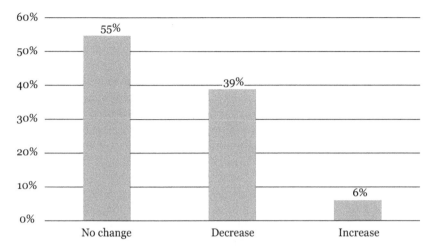

Figure 5.13   Impact of 2008 recession – enrollment

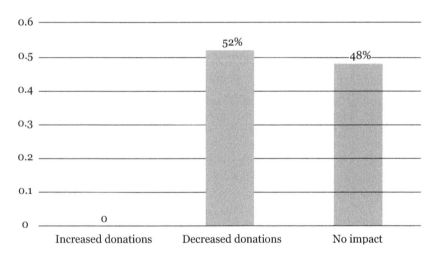

Figure 5.14   Impact of 2008 recession – donations

impact on donations and enrollment but not on volunteer hours (Figures 5.11–5.14).

It is not surprising that at times when Americans (including Muslim Americans) were losing jobs, facing economic uncertainty and possible reduced income, Islamic schools' tuition and donations may have seemed a luxury.

ANALYSIS

The survey of Islamic schools suggests that leaders of these nonprofit organizations have followed similar policies that help them attain both internal and external legitimacy. The Islamic school policies have assisted them in attaining performance, market, bureaucratic and financial accountability. Performance and bureaucratic accountability would tend to have an impact on external legitimacy. Internal legitimacy would be dependent upon all four measures of accountability.

Islamic schools report that they perform better than other schools in their area. Nearly one-fifth of Islamic schools report that they have been able to attract non-Muslim students to their schools. Nearly four-fifths of Islamic schools report that they are accredited. A majority of Islamic schools hire certified and trained teachers. A majority of Islamic schools report lower teacher–student ratios than traditional schools. All of these measures are ways in which Islamic schools have sought to attain strong performance measures that will lead to improved confidence in parents seeking to enroll children and donors seeking to support the school.

Islamic schools have also sought to pursue ways in which to fulfill market accountability. Almost all the schools in our survey report that their Islamic identity is important to them, with a few saying that they are schools run by Muslims in an effort to avoid being stereotyped. These schools seek to show themselves as a Muslim or Islamic alternative to traditional public and private schools. The majority of Islamic schools report that they have significant religious education as part of their curriculum while all report some sort of Islamic education. Nearly three-quarters of Islamic schools report that they receive support from the Muslim community. A large majority of Islamic schools also report that they have a formal curriculum. All of these measures seek to convey that Islamic schools have identified Muslim American parents as their primary market. They also suggest that Islamic schools seek to convey their ability to promote a sense of Islamic identity and a strong religious education in addition to a quality education equal to that that they would receive in a non-religious school as their main offering to these parents.

Islamic schools have sought to use accreditation as an important measure of bureaucratic accountability. In addition, the engaging of elected and non-elected board members as important ambassadors has further assisted in this process. Only 8 percent of Islamic schools report that they have a permanent board. The vast majority report that their board is subject to change. This constant engagement of new community members to the Islamic school boards increases oversight as well as the number of people who can vouch for the Islamic schools' ability to provide a quality education, transparent management and a sense of Islamic identity.

Finally, Islamic schools provide formal reports, reporting extensively to the community, state or local authority, a religious body or an accrediting agency. Only 9 percent state that they do not provide any kind of reporting. Furthermore, nearly 60 percent report that they receive some form of government support, suggesting the ability to comply with government accountability and reporting mechanisms.

CONCLUSION

Along with Islamic centers, Islamic schools in the US have become an important symbol of Muslim American institution building. While Islamic schools only educate less than 4 percent of Muslim American children, they have received both support and criticism. Internally, some Muslim Americans argue that Islamic schools create ghettos and take children away from a diverse American culture. Externally, some argue that Islamic schools are proponents of extremism. There is little definitive data to suggest that either of these two assertions are accurate.

However, this study, along with previous studies of Islamic schools, suggests that Islamic schools are taking the necessary steps to achieve legitimacy. The surveys suggest that suburban, middle-class, immigrant Islamic schools have taken specific programmatic, governance and operation steps to attain legitimacy within the Muslim American community. Islamic schools confirm previous research that suggests that 9/11 had no negative impact on philanthropic resources and legitimacy. On the other hand, Islamic schools, like many American nonprofits, found the Great Recession challenging and saw a decline in their philanthropic resources.

NOTES

1. ISNA Annual Report (1990).
2. For more on ISNA, see Siddiqui (2014).
3. "Muslim Americans Condemn Attack," available at http://www.islamicity.com/articles/Articles.asp?ref=AM0109-335 (accessed July 28, 2017).
4. *Islamic Horizons* (November/December 2001) p. 9.
5. "Muslim Americans Condemn Attack."
6. Our survey includes the zip code for each respondent school. The next step in this process would be to examine available test score data from the departments of education in various states to confirm this assertion.

REFERENCES

Asad, T. (1986), "The Idea of an Anthropology of Islam," Working paper series, Washington, DC: Center for Contemporary Arab Studies, Georgetown University.

Candler, G.G. (2001), "Transformations and Legitimacy in Nonprofit Organizations: The Case of Amnesty International and the Brutalization Thesis," *Public Organization Review*, 1 (3), 355–370.

Curtis, E.E., IV (2009), *Muslims in America: A Short History*. New York: Oxford University Press.

GhaneaBassiri, K. (2010), *A History of Islam in America*. Cambridge: Cambridge University Press.

Grewal, Z.A. and R.D. Coolidge (2013), "Islamic Education in the United States: Debates, Practices, and Institutions," in Juliane Hammer and Omid Safi (eds.), *The Cambridge Companion to American Islam*. New York: Cambridge University Press, pp. 246–265.

Haddad, Y., F. Senai and J.I. Smith (eds.) (2009), *Educating the Muslims of America*. Oxford: Oxford University Press.

Hanley, D. (2000), "Historic Muslim- and Arab-American Bloc Vote a Coveted Political Prize," *Washington Report of Middle East Affairs*, December 2000, p. 6.

Jeavons, T.H. (1992), "When the Management Is the Message: Relating Values to Management Practice in Nonprofit Organizations," *Nonprofit Management and Leadership*, 2 (4), 403–417.

Keyworth, K. (2009), "Islamic Schools of America," in Yvonne Haddad, Farid Senzai and Jane I. Smith (eds.), *Educating the Muslims of America*. Oxford: Oxford University Press, pp. 21–39.

Keyworth, K. (2011), *ISPU Report: Islamic Schools of the United States: Data-Based Profiles*. Dearborn, MI: Institute for Social Policy and Understanding.

Merry, M.S. and G. Driessen (2005), "Islamic Schools in Three Western Countries: Policy and Procedure," *Comparative Education*, 41 (4), 411–432.

Mosteller, F. (1995), "The Tennessee Study of Class Size in the Early School Grades," *The Future of Children*, 5 (2), 113–127.

Oseewaarde, R., A. Nijhof and L.Heyse (2008), "Dynamics of NGO Legitimacy: How Organising Betrays Core Missions of INGOs," *Public Administration and Development*, 28 (1), 42–53.

Ostrander, S.A. and P.G. Schervish (1990), "Giving and Getting: Philanthropy as a Social Relation," in J. Van Til (ed.), *Critical Issues in American Philanthropy*. San Francisco, CA: Jossey Bass, pp. 67–98.

Paino, M., L.A. Renzulli, R.L. Boyland and C.L. Bradley (2014), "For Grades or Money? Charter School Failure in North Carolina," *Educational Administration Quarterly*, 50 (3), 500–536.

Perko, M.F. (2000), "Religious Schooling in America: An Historiographical Reflection," *History of Education Quarterly*, 40 (3), 320–338.

Siddiqui, S. (2010), "Giving in the Way of God: Muslim Philanthropy in the United States," in David H. Smith (ed.), *Religious Giving: For Love of God*. Bloomington, IN: Indiana University Press.

Siddiqui, S.A. (2014), *Navigating Identity through Philanthropy: A History of the Islamic Society of North America (1979–2008)*. PhD Dissertation, Indiana University.

Suchman, Mark C. (1995), "Managing Legitimacy: Strategic and Institutional Approaches," *Academic of Management Review*, 20 (3), 571–610.

Vergari, Sandra (2007), "The Politics of Charter Schools," *Educational Policy*, 21 (1), 15–39.

Walker, E.T. and J.D. McCarthy (2010), "Legitimacy, Strategy, and Resources in the Survival of Community-Based Organizations," *Social Problems*, 57 (August), 315–340.

Zucker, L.G. (1987), "Institutional Theories of Organization," *Annual Review of Sociology*, 13 (1), 443–464.

6. Interlocutors of tradition or signposts of the future of Islam in America? Islamic schools in the US

INTRODUCTION

Towards the end of September 2016, a Michigan-based school won a $1.7 million lawsuit against the Michigan township of Pittsfield for unlawfully denying the Michigan Islamic Academy (MIA) the right to build on its property.[1] This news is significant, partly because of the fact that this case is one of the first of its kind, where a Muslim American institution has overcome resistance to Islamophobia. This news should be seen in the context of the Sterling Heights, MI controversy that erupted in 2016 when a mosque was denied permission to build its structure as there was local opposition.[2] The party that is at the center of dispute there, the American Islamic Community Center, has filed a lawsuit against the Planning Commission, accusing it of being discriminatory. With over 2000 mosques in the US and a growing Muslim community that is increasingly being seen as the most diverse of its kind in the US, the challenges to institution building are still prevalent, if these media reports are an indication (Bagby, 2011; Pew Research Center, 2012).

Researchers have studied Islamic education in the US from various perspectives. While there have been edited volumes that looked at this space in a holistic way (Haddad et al., 2009), there have also been attempts to look at the education (both secular and religious) of Muslim Americans through the public school systems and madrasas, or religious institutions and their linkages to global discourses of Islam (Grewal, 2013). As Haddad et al. point out, religious education of Muslims has been the province of the private realm of individuals, who have strived to "discern the best ways for both children and adults to learn and maintain the faith and practice of Islam" (2009, p. 10). This is especially pronounced in a secular society such as the US, where religious instruction in Islam is not possible in the public school system and avenues for socialization for Muslim American kids are few and far between. The public school system presents a unique challenge for those families that want to integrate, yet retain some of the traditional religious and cultural teachings that form the core of their identity.

Other studies that have sought to look at the institutional evolution of Muslim American institutions include that by Siddiqui, whose historical analysis of the Islamic Society of North America (ISNA) is one of the few that shed light on this aspect (Siddiqui, 2014). Siddiqui's analysis lays bare the changes that the most important Muslim American institution has had to go through to be accepted as the legitimate representative of the Muslim American community. Siddiqui's key argument, which is of use here, is that this paradigmatic institution has had to move from the relative isolationism that characterized the Muslim American community to what he calls a "culturally plural" model of governance and existence. As he argues, "America's acceptance of ISNA as the single Muslim American identity over others came at a heavy price – racial, ethnic, and ideological segregation" (2014, p. 2). In other words, this unidimensional representation of Muslim Americans as one entity is a problem, but one that has had to be created more out of a pragmatic necessity rather than by any consensus. This is also an example of how Muslim Americans translated their faith into practice, and one can make the same argument for Muslim American educational institutions.

The story of Muslim American educational institutions starts with the early missionaries from Asia, the Nation of Islam (NOI) and the recent immigrants who came post the 1965 Hart–Cellar Act, which made immigration from Asia and Middle East possible by removing the racial ban on non-White people. At the same time, the pioneering work of the NOI in establishing the University of Islam in Detroit should be seen for what it was – a firm attempt at rooting Islamic education in the US through formal institutional mechanisms (Haddad et al., 2009). While this followed the establishment of the Clara Muhammad Schools in the US, of which there were 41 at their peak, the numbers dropped with the separation of NOI, which Imam Warith Deen Muhammad brought about in 1978 when he split from the group to join mainstream Sunni Islam, taking a large number of his followers with him.

Karen Keyworth has written about the role of the Islamic Schools League of America (ISLA) in helping shape the curriculum of many of these schools in order to retain their spiritual integrity while remaining "mainstream" in their focus (Keyworth, 2009). She has estimated that there are roughly 32 000 students in full-time Islamic schools. She further points to the debates going on in these schools regarding some of the many issues that are ongoing in the public school system too – bullying, certification and dropout rates, graduation rates and so on. Keyworth has also argued that it is indeed hard to know the exact number of Islamic schools that are present in the US, and that is a fair point given that many of the schools have moved locations, and a few have closed down or merged with other schools. In our own research, we found that it is very hard to pin down the exact number. But based on our aggregation of the schools' addresses, email IDs and other identification parameters, we have come up with the number that we use in this chapter and elsewhere.

On a related note, as Ihsan Bagby's research on the growth of American mosques has shown, the growth of Islamic centers is closely tied to the growth and evolution of Islamic schools, as in most cases they either share the governing board or have common origins. Given that the number of mosques/Islamic centers in the US is close to 2000 now, this growth can also be attributed to the growth of Islamic schools, as they are institutions of cultural and intellectual socialization (Bagby, 2011). Bagby's survey counted 2106 mosques, and our survey found a total of 230 Islamic schools, meaning that about 10 percent of the mosques had an Islamic school in the community.

In this context of increased attention to Muslim communities and their practices, Muslim American communities have had to deal with the issue of representation as much as focusing on building their own communities of practice (Ahmad, 2012). Ahmad talks about the diversity of religious instruction and practices, within the umbrella of Islamic studies, taught at Islamic schools. While there are Muslims from all over the world in the US, it does create unique challenges in terms of both pedagogy and understanding of how these practices should be enforced, given that each school of thought has a slightly different way of interpreting Islamic law. This is also especially interesting and unique in the case of African American Muslims, who come with a somewhat uniquely American perspective given the history of African Americans in the US who have converted to Islam; many of them entered Islam through the NOI.

In the case of African American Muslims, or the Historically Sunni African American Muslims (HSAAMs) as Siddiqui calls them, these schools have a slightly different focus – that is, preserving and promoting the cultural identity as Black Muslims, who have had not only to survive the devastating effects of slavery in the US, but also overcome racial animosities which continue to this day.[3] If the Black Lives Matter movement is an indication of the rawness of this emotion, then the racial healing that was supposed to happen post-Civil Rights Movement hasn't occurred fully (Curtis, 2009).

The Clara Muhammad Schools have been predominantly engaged in educating African American Muslim children and also attract a large number of non-Muslim children. Given their focus on character building, discipline and developing good morals, these schools have been perceived as important in their communities. As Merry and Driessen (2005) point out, they operate under the motto of "intelligence without morality is a destructive force." The same problems that characterize other Islamic schools face these schools too, which try to be seen as "Islamic" (Hakim and Muhammad, 1992). In addition to the problems that characterize African Americans generally, the African American Muslim schools also face the dual problem of dealing with technical issues such as lack of technical expertise in fundraising and integration in the formal world of foundations, private donor relations and so on.

While the discourse of Islam in America is occurring in the context of assimilation, integration and challenges to Muslims in the public sphere, there is another parallel discussion of Islam in the world that impinges on this, rather diametrically. This is one of global discourses of Islam and Islamic education. Looking at the comparative aspects of Islamic education, Merry and Driessen have looked at how Islamic schools in the US compare to schools in the Netherlands and Belgium. They suggest that higher academic standards and a more morally acceptable environment are the main draws for Muslim parents to admit their children to Islamic schools (Merry and Driessen, 2005). The rise of the rhetoric of political Islam in parts of the world and the concomitant rise of ethnic profiling has necessitated the need for creating a more positive Islamic identity in the West, and these schools aim to do that. In Belgium, there has been resistance to Islamic schools, they point out, reflecting a trend that is somewhat present in the US, though the exercise of the First Amendment allows Muslim Americans to establish their faith-based schools. Our argument is that it is possible to provide an Islamic education without getting into the intricacies of political Islam or even without partaking in the ideological minefield of Islamism or Islam in the public sphere.

Merry and Driessen also point to the fact that since Islamic schools borrow heavily from their surroundings, both from public schools and private ones, there is an internal perception among the schools that there is little difference between them and the others, except for a dress code, Islamic practices and so on. The story of the overworked, underpaid school administrator in an Islamic school is all too common, they point out, acknowledging that the average tenure of such an administrator is three years in Islamic schools, while it is six years in a public school setting (Maughan, 2003). Some of these issues are discussed in this chapter as well. While there are stark differences in the way Islamic schools are run, we suggest that the commonalities between them and other private schools are too extensive to be ignored.

Further, as Merry and Driessen point out, just because the state apparatus does not interfere in the workings of the faith-based schools doesn't mean that they are running these schools in any manner that works for them, but rather they solicit feedback from others – public officials, other schools and also the local communities – in order to bring their work on a par with other schools. Competition and cooperation are themes that emerge in this story as well. The US seems unique in that there are private schools, while in the Netherlands and Belgium they don't exist, despite constitutional guarantees. This may be because of the unique way in which the American nonprofit sector has evolved and grown, offering a vibrant space for civil society to contribute to education, healthcare and other core sectors of American society.

METHOD

The present chapter incorporates insights and perspectives from the participants in the research and develops a theory, based on data, following a constructivist Grounded Theory approach, as advocated by Charmaz (2013). In this sense, the validity and reliability of responses can be determined using several approaches. One of them is to focus on "viability" (utility) of responses, rather than purely focusing on validity (truth), as several scholars have pointed out (Neimeyer and Neimeyer, 1993, p. 2; Morrow and Smith, 1995).

We also used interviews to triangulate data and categories, especially if the interviewees were not entirely forthcoming. While interviews are to be taken at face value, a closer examination of extant documents such as annual reports, media reports of certain incidents and other scholarly analysis of certain themes, which we could not explore in-depth due to the sensitive nature of the topic, helped us gain a fuller understanding of the "code" or theme under consideration.

Data collection also included visits to some of the schools where possible and participating in some of the activities – fundraisers, speeches given by key administrators – during important occasions. We attended forums such as annual conventions of the ISNA and the ISNA Education Forum held in Chicago in 2016.

We used Constructivist Grounded Theory as our primary method of investigation. In this method, which is rooted in the approach that Kathy Charmaz has proposed, reality is constructed by the researcher and not "out there" in the data or the analysis. Charmaz has built this approach using a symbolic interactionist theoretical perspective. As she argues, "We construct our grounded theories through our past and present involvements and interactions with people, perspectives and research practices" (2013, p. 17). This also means that the approach Charmaz suggests is flexible, and not a rigid set of rules, recipes and requirements. We have followed this approach in our interviews, which were conducted using a snowball sampling method given that many of the principals and board members were able to refer us to other colleagues, who offered feedback and gave us the opportunity to interview them.

PARTICIPANTS

We managed to secure 20 semi-structured interviews with principals, board members and other key administrators of the schools, spread across the Greater Washington DC area, New York metro area, Chicago metro area, Southern California with a few in Georgia and Tennessee. The participants included both men and women, ranging in age from their mid-30s to late 60s. The profile of the interviewees represented (though not intentionally) the full range of diversity that is present in the Muslim American communities – Asian, African American, Arab, Caucasian and other ethnic minorities. Almost all of them had worked in the Islamic schools system for a substantial amount of time, though some were new to the role of administrator. Many had been promoted internally, from being teachers to being administrators, and they saw this as an opportunity to continue to contribute to the community's development and to their moral and professional obligation, both to their children (many of whom studied in these schools) and the community (and the country) at large.

TYPES OF ISLAMIC SCHOOLS

There are various types of institutions that cater to the education needs of Muslim Americans

- Full-time Islamic schools
- Sunday schools that teach the Qur'an and Islamic studies
- Daycare centers
- Islamic tutoring centers that offer part-time instruction in some subjects
- Hifz schools that teach the students memorization of the Qur'an.

Siddiqui's framework of analyzing Muslim American groups as the "activists, HSAAMs (Historically Sunni African American Muslims), and cultural pluralists" is a good starting point for understanding, analytically, the vast diversity of Muslim American institutions (Siddiqui,

2014). While there are Muslims in the US who are from all parts of the world and from almost every country, the ideological and sectarian affiliations can be narrowed down to fewer than the number of countries that they come from. Beyond the simplistic Sunni versus Shii or Salafi versus Sufi terminologies, there can be a more nuanced approach to understanding the types of Islamic schools, and we aim to offer such a typology here.

PROCEDURE

The participants in this research were recruited from the sample database we created, which aimed to map the entire universe of the Islamic Schools in the US (full-time schools only). We did not include schools that were operated on a part-time basis (Sunday schools) or provided purely religious instruction (Hifz schools), simply because comparing them with public schools and other parochial schools would not have been possible. In addition, we chose schools that were at least two years old, to ensure that there were some procedures and processes established and that the school had survived the initial stages following set-up.

We sent out emails with details of the research questions and related recruiting material over several LISTSERVS, in addition to reaching out through our database of contacts. Participants who elected to participate were given the necessary documentation and disclosure material before being interviewed over the phone or, in some cases, in person. The interviews varied from 60 to 90 minutes; responses were recorded and transcribed by us.

DATA SOURCES

Each of the participants took part in a semi-structured interview with largely open-ended questions. We asked a few questions related to the organizational structure, such as "Is your school affiliated with a mosque?"; "Does that offer you credibility and legitimacy?"; "What portion of your operating revenues are from philanthropy?"; and "How important is the local community's volunteering in running your school?" We also probed identity aspects with open-ended questions such as "How much of your syllabus would be considered 'Islamic'" and "What are the 'Islamic values' that you imbue in your students?" We discussed aspects of consent and confidentiality before the call was set up/commenced. Each participant agreed to participate in the publication of the work in the hope that it would create a more nuanced understanding of Islamic schools, among both scholars and the general public.

Additional data came in the form of participant observation at the ISNA Educational Forum as well as at the annual ISNA conferences. We were able to participate in the events and gather insights from the discussions, panels and informal discussions with board members/governing members of the Islamic schools who were present at both venues. Finally, the third major source of data was the rich repertoire of insights from Siddiqui, who has played a key role in establishing the ISLA, and also from the self-reflection journal that Khan kept throughout the research efforts.

DATA COLLECTION, ANALYSIS AND WRITING

Once the data were recorded, we transcribed them, verbatim. In some cases, notes included insights garnered from participant observation in a meeting at a school – we were able to access a handful of schools throughout this research project – and also in meetings with the board members of the schools at other venues, as mentioned earlier. The entire corpus of data was shared between us in an attempt to come to a mutual understanding of the data available and also to start the analytical process of synthesizing and gleaning what is important from what is not.

We analyzed and immersed ourselves in the data as well as compared notes. The analytical process began with open coding, with an attempt to try to understand the categories, or "buckets" of information, that could be formed, or the themes that could emerge, going through data line by line. This followed a pattern of coding for *initial, focused and selective coding*. Open codes are those that "fracture the data and allow one to identify some categories, their properties and their different dimensional locations" (Strauss and Corbin, 1990, quoted in Morrow and Smith, 1995, p. 26). Some of the codes that emerged were also *in vivo* codes, or those used by participants to refer to certain ideas and concepts. Two of these were "Islamic identity" and "Islamic values." We used their self-reflective memos to understand this process and also triangulated this by going back to the interviewees and asking them what they meant specifically when they used these terms.

Focused or axial coding followed. This involved comparing codes and making connections between categories (Charmaz, 2013). The next stage was selective coding, which is an integrative stage which relates to other categories, validating those relationships and also looking for confirming or disconfirming information. This also includes "filling in categories that need further refinement and development" (Strauss and Corbin, 1990, p. 116).

The final stage involved theory development, which entailed making sure that there was theoretical saturation in terms of codes. This means that new analysis does not produce any new codes or categories. As Strauss points out, some of the criteria for core status in grounded theory include (1) category's centrality in relation to other categories, (2) frequency of a category's occurrence, (3) inclusiveness and ease with which it relates to other categories, (4) clarity and implications for theory, (5) movement towards theoretical power and (6) allowance for maximum variation in terms of dimensions, properties, conditions, consequences and strategies (Strauss, 1987).

To ensure that the research was representative of the views of those researched and was valid, we conducted "member-checking," that is, showing preliminary drafts of the chapter to the participants and seeking feedback in terms of the categories that were created and the analysis itself. Their feedback was included to help clarify and correct any analytical misinterpretations that we may have made. This procedure has been recommended by several researchers including Fine (1992) and Morrow and Smith (1995).

RESULTS

The Grounded Theory model for growth and evolution of Islamic schools is presented in Figure 6.1.

Theorizing the Growth of Islamic Schools in the US

From the data gathered and initial, focused and selective coding, we begin to find themes that start to explain, at an analytical level, what is going on. To form a theory of the evolution of these institutions, in order to explain the phenomenon under study, we propose a model below.

Causal Conditions Related to Founding and Proliferation of Islamic Schools

Throughout the interviews several causal conditions emerged that demonstrate the perceived need for Islamic schools. Some of the key ones include (1) perception of lack of Islamic socialization in immigrant communities, (2) poor quality public schools and (3) need for preserving tradition/religious values.

Immigrant communities

Many of the identity aspects emerge when these communities are perceived as, or indeed are, immigrant communities with either first- or second-generation Muslim Americans. While their roots in the US, through citizenship or work, are being formed, their ties to their country of origin are still strong.

For instance, for one school in Tennessee, the plan was for the school to be built within the mosque's architecture when the initial planning and discussions were being held. But later on, the board decided to keep the school in a separate structure, adjacent to the mosque, with its own board and management structure. This means that the local community felt the need for such a school with a strong religious curriculum. Speaking to the challenges of sustaining such schools, the principal pointed out:

> We go from year to year, surviving. Thank god, with this approach too, there is great deal of stability and over the past 25 years I did not see many schools close, just one or two and there are other factors for their closure. Usually they don't close completely and they convert to different location and it's not like foreclosure because they don't have support. Islamic schools in general face the dual identity – when I talk about the identity the question whether we are Muslim or American.

On further probing, he revealed that this dual identity is not really an impediment to them constructing their own identity as an organization that serves both the community and the nation at large, by producing citizens who are law-abiding and contributing members of the society.

He further pointed out that:

> Generally speaking, the dual identity has also developed over the years. Now, most of the schools claim that we are Americans and Muslims and they don't contradict and have same priority – to work for interest of nation and family, to raise kids as Muslims. Generally, Islamic schools have, you know, the fear of the political situation in America.

Poor quality public schools

The second main reason why Islamic schools are created is because parents feel there are not many good quality public schools. As one board member of a school in Columbia, MD explained

> Most of us in this community are highly educated people, some with PhDs and Masters degrees, and there is a perception among some parents, well many in fact, that the public school system here leaves much to be desired. The fact that we want our kids to do well is what motivated many of us to come together and start a school. It was as much a pragmatic decision, as it was one rooted in our own felt need for greater control of our kids' education.

So, rooted in this desire to help their children get a quality education is the motive to have some element of control over how their children behave during the day, what sorts of activities they take part in, and the peers that they spend time with.

Need for preserving tradition/religious values

One of the most important reasons/causal conditions for establishing Islamic schools is the need for preserving religious values. As with other parochial schools, there is a wide variation in the practices of Islam, but through the interviews, almost all the principals and board members also pointed out that the environment in which the children study is very important for them.

As one principal of a school, who is also the founder, pointed out:

> My child was in Islamic schools, till KG, from Pre-K. I had given up my job at George Washington University, and worked in the Islamic school to be with him. When he made it to KG, I stated that this is not what I want for my own child. He deserves better environment and many other ways you can educate them, rather than a rigid environment. This alternative came across and I started on this project of starting a new school.

Of the principals and board members interviewed, almost all had some sort of experience that involved their own children and the perceived need for their education to be Islamic. The key motivating factor for these parents to get involved in either starting an Islamic school or serving in one was the desire to help their own children have a better "Islamic environment" and also help other kids to benefit from such an environment.

Phenomena Resulting from the Causal Conditions

The growth in number of Islamic schools is a direct result of the above-mentioned causal conditions. While the actual growth has been slow, and in some cases schools have shut down or consolidated with others, the reasons for this are mixed.

Growth/evolution of Islamic schools

There has been a slow and steady growth in the number of Islamic schools. This is a result of both perceived and felt need and also the growing number of mosques in the US (see our reference to the mosque study by Dr. Ihsan Bagby). The growth of Islamic schools, though not directly related, in all cases is definitely impacted by the number of mosques. As mentioned earlier, many of the schools begin within a mosque and gradually expand

and outgrow the mosque, both physically and also in terms of governing structure – board control and so on.

Philanthropic support

In almost all cases, the financial support to start the school, or the capital, has come from a core group of supporters or a family. This means that philanthropy plays a crucial role in the founding of the institution. The capital may also come from the local mosque if it decides to support the school or, in some cases, start the school in its own premises.

The other possibility is that the school emerges organically from a Sunday school program and slowly outgrows the existing structure. The role of philanthropy in Islamic schools is rather complicated and is not linear. In many cases, the community's support remains firmly with the school, while in some other cases the philanthropic support – in terms of both money and volunteering – varies depending on the awareness of such actions among these parents, as one principal pointed out. She said:

> In some cases, we have received money from non-Muslim parents of children who are with us, and Muslim parents don't donate as much. It may be because many of these parents think that once they pay fees, their job is done; while the non-Muslim parents don't think about it this way. They see the school as contributing to the community, at large. I have noticed this through my work in the local community.

Context

The context in which the Islamic schools continue to grow is also important to consider. In some cases, there is active resistance to these schools, both from within the Muslim community and from the larger community, while in many (or most) cases, there has been a lot of support – from both Muslims and non-Muslims living in the town/community.

Religious obligation/civic duty

The obligation to preserve "Islamic teachings" is one of the main contextual factors. In an environment that is decidedly secular in outlook and has strong Christian morality infused in public life, many of the principals of schools pointed out that preserving Islamic values of modesty, honesty, obedience to parents and so on were what prompted them to consider Islamic schools. The obligation to serve the community and also do good for the country was often cited as another factor that contributed to their participation in the Islamic schools network.

Need for more quality education
Many of the school principals also pointed to the high number of students in classrooms and the teacher–student ratio as being problematic. As one parent board member said,

> I find it hard to believe that a teacher who has to attend to 35 students in a class can do a good job of teaching my daughter. I chose an Islamic school for my daughter because the teacher–student ratio is very good, with just 10–12 students per class. My daughter would not only get to know the teacher better, but also form deeper relationships with her peers. I think this sort of bonding is very important for students, at a young age.

This sentiment was reflected by a majority of the 20 principals/board members interviewed, who all had their children in Islamic schools, either at the time of the interview or in the recent past.

Bullying in public schools
Another persistent theme that came up during the interviews, and one that could contribute as a contextual factor, is that of bullying in public schools. With the heightened threat of Islamic terrorism and increased discourse of Islam in the public sphere, many kids have started to bully others, especially using the epithet of "terrorist" and so on. This has added to the fear among some parents that their kids would be bullied if they were to be part of a system that may see them as "distinct" or "inherently different." The desire to have some control over this sort of bullying prompted them to choose Islamic schools for their children.

Intervening Conditions

There have been several intervening conditions that have played a role in how these schools perceive their own position in American society and for their continued existence. Some of the key ones include the following.

Post-9/11 rhetoric of Islam
The perception of Islam and Muslims in the US has unfortunately been negative since the terrorist attacks of 9/11.[4] Opinion polls taken recently, by organizations such as Gallup and Pew, point to a bleak picture, where more than 43 percent of Americans had some sort of prejudiced view of Muslims. As the Gallup report points out, "Prejudice toward Muslims was higher than self-reported prejudice toward any of the various religious groups tested." This factor has to be taken into account when understanding the self-perceived threats that Muslim Americans feel and also the actual reality of dealing with these prejudices.

Islamophobia

Islamophobia – both perceived and real – was mentioned repeatedly as a factor that has forced some parents to put their children in Islamic schools. Related to the point above, they felt that some parts of mainstream society do not understand "true Islam," and this sheltering of their children from these elements was necessary, to secure both their physical and their psychological wellbeing.

US Elections cycle (local and national)

Some of the interviewees mentioned that the rhetoric about Islam and Islamic schools tends to be negative particularly around election cycles. As one principal of a school in Indianapolis pointed out, "In particular, this year has been bad and we hope that the negative rhetoric comes down, so people don't focus on the negative stereotypes about us or our schools." This sense of feeling persecuted by the political apparatus was visible among many of the principals and other board members of these schools.

Strategies

The schools have adopted several strategies to deal with the perceived and real prejudice (in some cases) from some segments of society.

Inclusiveness

Most schools have a very inclusive approach to who can study at their schools. About half of the schools have non-Muslim students, while the others have an open door policy, but don't have non-Muslims as students. This also means that there are students from different denominations – Sunni, Shii or Ahmadiyyas, at their schools. As one principal pointed out, "We may have students who are Muslims, who may not participate in the Islamic studies classes or Arabic as it is not mandatory for all students. In that sense, we have an inclusive community of students, though our identity is strongly Islamic." This sense of inclusiveness has helped some of the schools keep open spaces for both Muslim and non-Muslim students to participate in and be part of the community.

Integrating in mainstream

To tackle the misconception that these schools are "different" or breed an "exceptional" mindset, the focus of many of these schools has been on integrating with the "mainstream" of education – either through adopting the state curriculum standards or the International Baccalaureate (IB) curriculum – to keep them on par with international standards. In almost all interviews, the focus was on ensuring that students graduated with skills

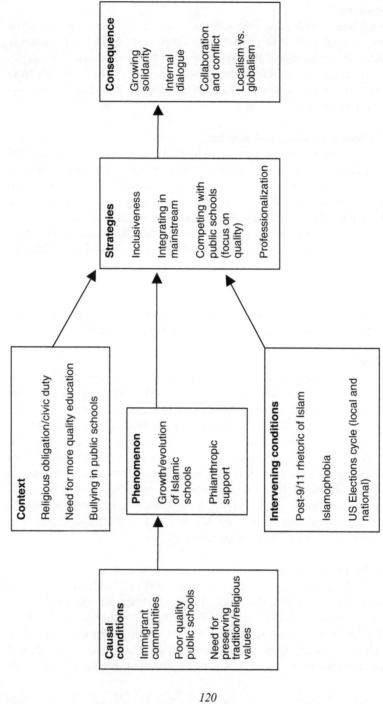

Figure 6.1   Growth and evolution of Islamic schools – a model based on Grounded Theory analysis[5]

that would help them integrate into regular mainstream schools/technical institutes.

Professionalization

There is also a growing focus on professionalization, given the demands from parents that teachers keep up with those teachers in the public school systems. This means that many of the schools apply for Title I, II grants, for professional development. "Even though it takes a lot of paper work, I apply for some of the grant money from the DoE as it helps us with training our staff etc., which is very important," pointed out an administrator.

Consequences

The strategies adopted by the schools and the principals of schools had a range of consequences from more solidarity internally to greater negotiation among the board members and other stakeholders.

Growing solidarity

There is a growing sense of solidarity among those who send their children to these Islamic schools, pointed out one principal. This means that the Muslim community is bound together not only at the Islamic center, where they gather for prayers, social events and so on, but also in developing a greater sense of community solidarity.

Internal dialogue

"The amount of internal dialogue within the community is also increasing," pointed out another board member. This occurs in various instances, when there is either feedback solicited from parents or someone new at the school. "Even during fund-raisers, we get feedback from parents on various issues and this is a healthy trend. While some parents are totally hands-off, we do get very good feedback and push-back also, from some parents. This sort of internal dialogue about what our schools mean to the community is important," she pointed out.

Collaboration and conflict

While schools collaborate with each other, there is also scope for conflict with other Islamic schools in the area or with the mosque board. While the most common source of collaboration was over fundraising and so on, the source of conflict was the same, along with perceived "micro-management" of the processes by the schools' board. As one founding principal pointed out, speaking about the relationship with the local mosque, "We are not mosque affiliated and hope we will not be. Being affiliated with a mosque limits the organization and my observation of other schools and education centers. Our main goal is education and we would like to keep it as that. I don't want any other factors to affect that."

Localism versus globalism
In many cases, the real tension is between building an identity that is rooted in a completely "American" identity and building one which connects with global discourses of Islam. This is a real tension that many schools are working out. While this tension does not play out in the day-to-day functioning of the school, the aspects of how Islam should be taught do come up – for instance, in terms of prayers and so on. As one school principal pointed out, "When we have two kids who pray slightly differently, because they are from different *madhab*, we try to find a common ground, and tell them that the differences are very minor and should not be cause for tension."

DISCUSSION

While the literature on Islamic schools examines aspects of pedagogy, Islamic identity and so on, there is not much on the institutional dimensions of what makes a school "Islamic" and what factors have contributed to the growth and evolution of such institutions. Our work aims to fill this gap in the literature.

Our model tries to offer this analysis, based on the perceptions and ideas of those key stakeholders who frame the discourse of Islamic schools in the US: the principals and board members of these institutions.

As one can see from Figure 6.2, the role of philanthropy varies, from

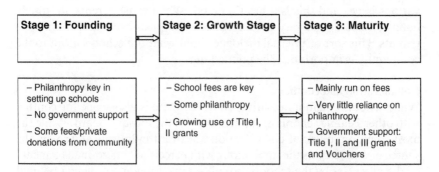

Figure 6.2   Growth of Islamic schools and reliance on community philanthropy

being crucial and foundational in the beginning stages to being almost insignificant in the later stages, once the school matures.

Societal conditions impact the growth and evolution of any school, whether it is Islamic or otherwise, and in this case we see that while there is a lot of support among the general public, sometimes resistance to these schools comes from surprising quarters. It could be from the town council, as we saw at the beginning of this chapter, or from the Muslim community itself, which doesn't want to "ghettoize" its youth by cutting them off from mainstream society. But as the interviews show, and a closer examination of the dynamics of these schools points to, there is an overwhelming effort on the part of the principals to integrate the students in "mainstream" American society – through the curriculum, trips to the local institutions of government or other extracurricular activities.

One must not underestimate the amount of resolve and dedication that many of these principals and board members bring by virtue of their sacrifices. Many of them give up lucrative careers in the private sector or in the public school system to serve in these schools, often with the sole intention of serving the community and their children. This, combined with the lower salary scales in many of these institutions, makes working in these schools a real challenge.

NOTES

1. For more, see "Islamic School Awarded $1.7 Million in Settlement of CAIR-MI Suit against Michigan Township," available at http://lenamasri.com/post/151103583349/islamic-school-awarded-17-million-in-settlement (accessed February 2017).
2. For more, see "Lawsuit Filed over Denial of Mosque in Sterling Heights," available at http://www.detroitnews.com/story/news/local/macomb-county/2016/08/10/sterling-hei ghts-mosque/88527210/ (accessed February 2017).
3. Based on interview with a consultant and advisory member of the Clara Muhammad Schools, who has worked with Imam Warith Deen Muhammad.
4. For more, see "Perceptions of Muslims in the United States: A Review," http://www.gallup.com/opinion/gallup/187664/perceptions-muslims-united-states-review.aspx (accessed February 2017).
5. Model's guiding framework is drawn from Morrow and Smith (1995).

REFERENCES

Ahmad, S.M. (2012), *Islamic Parochial Education in the United States: A Study of Two Atlanta-Area Schools*. Thesis, Georgia State University.

Bagby, I. (2011), *The American Mosque: Basic Characteristics of the American Mosque and Attitudes of Mosque*. Washington, DC: Council on American Islamic Relations.

Charmaz, K. (2013), *Constructing Grounded Theory: A Practical Guide through Qualitative Analysis*. Thousand Oaks, CA Sage Publications, Inc.

Curtis, E.E., IV (2009), *Muslims in America: A Short History*. New York: Oxford University Press.

Fine, M. (1992), *Disruptive Voices: The Possibilities of Feminist Research*. Ann Arbor, MI: University of Michigan Press.

Grewal, Z. (2013), *Islam Is a Foreign Country: Muslim Americans and the Global Crisis of Authority*. New York: New York University Press.

Haddad, Y., F. Senai and J.I. Smith (eds.) (2009), *Educating the Muslims of America*. New York: Oxford University Press.

Hakim, R. and Z. Muhammad (1992), "The Sister Clara Muhammad Schools: Pioneers in the Development of Islamic Education in America," *Journal of Negro Education*, 61 (2), 178–185.

Keyworth, K. (2009), "Islamic Schools in America: Data Profiles," in Yvonne Haddad, Farid Senai and Jane I. Smith (eds.), *Educating the Muslims of America*. Oxford University Press, pp. 15–28.

Maughan, E. (2003), The Impact of School Nursing on School Performance," *Journal of School Nursing*, 19 (3), 163–171.

Merry, M. and G. Driessen (2005), "Islamic Schools in Three Western Countries: Policy and Procedure," *Comparative Education*, 41 (4), 411–432.

Morrow, S.L. and M.L. Smith (1995), "Constructions of Survival and Coping by Women Who Have Survived Childhood Sexual Abuse," *Journal of Counseling and Psychology*, 42 (1), 24–33.

Neimeyer, G.J. and R.A. Neimeyer (1993), "Defining the Boundaries of Constructivist Assessment," in G.J. Neimeyer (ed.), *Constructivist Assessment: A Case Book*. Newbury Park, CA: Sage Publications, Inc., pp. 1–30.

Pew Research Center (2012), *The World's Muslims: Unity and Diversity*, Washington, DC: Pew Research Center.

Siddiqui, S.A. (2014), *Navigating Identity through Philanthropy: A History of the Islamic Society of North America (1979–2008)*. PhD Dissertation, Indiana University.

Strauss, A.L. (1987), *Qualitative Analysis for Social Sciences*. Cambridge: Cambridge University Press.

Strauss, A.L. and J.M. Corbin (1990), *Basics of Qualitative Research: Grounded Theory Approaches and Techniques*. Newbury Park, CA, Sage.

7. Conclusion: prospects for future growth and development

Islamic schools in America have been a controversial topic both within and outside the community. With renewed attention towards their functioning and the focus on "radicalism" in the Muslim community, we believe that these schools will receive more scrutiny in the years to come. However, there are prospects for change, as we have outlined in this book. While Islam in America is becoming accepted by mainstream Americans, there remain challenges to the full acceptance of Muslim institutions in the US.

The growth of Islamic schools is impacted by public perception of Muslims and Muslim institutions, as we saw in the previous chapters. While there have been supportive communities that have welcomed Islamic schools in their midst, there have also been many instances where there have been legal battles and challenges to the establishment of these schools. The recent incident in Michigan (see Chapter 6) is an example. The situation with respect to Muslim institutions in the US is dynamic and changing. A recent study mentioned by the Brookings Institution points out that the public perception of Islam seems to be moving to become more favorable.[1] As Shibley Telhami points out: "Attitudes towards Muslim people became progressively more favorable from 53 percent in November 2015 to 70 percent in October 2016." He goes on to argue that even attitudes towards Islam itself showed improvement and they were up from 37 percent in November 2015 to 49 percent in October 2016, reaching the highest favorable level since September 11, 2001. As Telhami explains, the shift was along partisan lines, there being a radical shift from 67 percent to 81 percent favorability among Democrats but not a perceptible movement among Republicans.

The public perception of Islam may shift more towards the positive as draconian laws are enacted and Muslim civil society is under threat – whether real or perceived. The fact that there is a bill in the US Congress that is attempting to designate the Muslim Brotherhood a "terrorist" organization is a worry that is very real and urgent. This designation means that many of the domestic organizations such as the Islamic Society of North America (ISNA) and Council on American–Islamic Relations (CAIR) would be considered "Muslim Brotherhood affiliates" by the logic of the arguments that have been put forward. Designating these as terrorist organizations would deal a deadly blow to the Muslim American institutional framework, given that these are some of the most important national organizations that have advocated, and continue to advocate, civic engagement of Muslim Americans.

While the Trump administration has made claims about cracking down on "radical Islam," the recent rebranding of the Countering Violent Extremism (CVE) program to "Countering Violent Islamic Radicalism" is being seen as a move to put the focus only on Islam; a move that is as problematic in tone as it is in its implications. There have been concerns about the advisors that President Trump has gathered, in regard to issues related to Islam. The threats of Islamic radicalism domestically are being exaggerated, point out critics of the recent move by the Trump administration. This also means that there is a danger of the entire religion of Islam being branded as "radical."[2] As the authors of a report in the *New York Times* point out, there is a concern that some of the conspiracy theories about "Shariah Law" taking over the US and other similar theories are becoming mainstream. This climate of fear and shift in policy towards a religious group represents a real danger to both the freedom of speech and the way in which Muslim American institutions continue to function.

Among other things, the appointment of Lt. Gen. Michael T. Flynn as National Security Advisor, who was later forced to resign due to unrelated matters, was both alarming and deeply troubling for the Muslim community. He is on record as saying that Islam is not a religious system, but a political ideology that has religion as a component. This suggests that the very basis on which religious freedom is guaranteed in the US – that is, being defined as a religion – is under threat for Islam in the US.

Our starting point for our research, and indeed this book, was that Muslim philanthropy plays a key role in the founding and functioning of Islamic schools in the US. As we have seen, this working thesis has evolved. While it is true that philanthropy plays a key role in the founding of most of the Islamic schools, we have seen that in the long run the role of philanthropy diminishes – often with other sources of revenue playing a bigger role. For instance, revenue from fees takes an upper hand, and this is true in most cases. However, as our survey demonstrated, philanthropy remains an important source of revenues for these schools. This is especially true when considering volunteer hours and philanthropic legitimacy, which are both important to the schools.

The founders and administrators of Islamic schools perceive themselves as guardians of the best traditions of learning in the Muslim community. Given the high value placed on learning in traditional Muslim cultures, it is not surprising that they take their work seriously. Also, given that the founders of these schools are largely immigrants who are first, second or third generation Muslims, there is a focus on providing quality education that is comparable to the best private institutions, especially given that many of the parents of these kids are successful professionals – doctors, engineers, architects and other professionals with a clear idea of what is good for their children.

MUSLIM AMERICAN INSTITUTION BUILDING: WHAT CAN WE SAY WITH CERTAINTY?

As we pointed out in the chapters of this book, Muslim American institutions emerged over a period of time, primarily starting in the 1980s, when Muslims found deeper roots in the communities in which they lived. Gone were the days when Muslim Americans saw themselves as sojourners. They were here to stay and to claim their rights as citizens which came with guarantees of freedom of speech and all the concomitant rights. This is an important point to remember, as many of the immigrant communities came from contexts where free practice of religion was barred, especially if their version of Islam was different from the "mainstream" in that country. The case of the Ahmadiyya community from South Asia is a classic example of a community that has thrived in the US after being persecuted in their home countries for several decades.

As the previously discussed mosque survey by Dr. Ihsan Bagby has shown, the growth of Muslim American mosques is an indication of the growth of the Muslim American consciousness as well as the community's ability to maintain its traditional orthodox beliefs (Bagby, 2011). At the same time, the mosques have also become centers of creative interpretation of Islam and its cultural traditions. American mosques do not serve the same functions as mosques in other parts of the world.

Our research in the survey and interviews that followed also demonstrates that Muslim American institutions are evolving in relation to other institutions – borrowing the best practices and norms of other mainstream institutions. While there is direct collaboration in many cases, when it comes to issues of interfaith dialogue and so on, in some cases the influence of "mainstream" or secular institutions is more subtle. For instance, all Muslim American institutions have adopted the nonprofit form, which allows them to benefit from the system through deductibility on income tax filing.

WHAT HAVE WE LEARNED FROM THE STUDY?

This project also demonstrated to us that the debates within the Muslim American community of "assimilation versus isolation" are no longer as prevalent as they were just two decades ago. Muslim Americans, over the years, have chosen to integrate, while keeping their values intact. The model of "cultural pluralism" they have followed is that of Jewish groups that have, in the past, faced similar issues in the US (Siddiqui, 2014). While the patterns of integration have been different and continue to evolve, the challenges in relation to them have been similar.

While the original thesis that we started with, that Islamic schools are sites of culture preservation and transfer, holds true, it must be restated. The reformulated thesis, based on the data and analysis, might be stated as: Islamic schools are both the sites of transfer of knowledge, culture and traditions and the sites of contestation of values and norms of what it means to offer an "Islamic" education. As we have seen in the interviews, there is a continuum of what it means to be an "Islamic school" and how visible the "Islamic" element of the school should be. There seems to be a vast divergence in terms of how much each school wants to be perceived as "Islamic." While all the school principals agree that the values of honesty, integrity, collaboration, accountability and modesty are to be imparted, the degree of divergence is more on the issue of "branding" these values as being particular to Islamic institutions or whether theirs is a regular institution that follows these "Islamic values."

Let us look at each of the four dimensions across which we analyzed these schools: legitimacy, Islamic identity, public policy and leadership.

Legitimacy

While Islamic schools are continuing to gain legitimacy both internally (with the Muslim communities) and externally (with the state and the broader community), there is little doubt that they have come a long way. From the time that the first Muslim schools emerged in the US, through the Nation of Islam (NOI), which helped set up many of the Clara Muhammad Schools, there has been a gradual evolution of what these schools mean for the communities in which they are based, as well as for the nearby communities.

There has been a rapid evolution and transformation of both the management styles and the branding of these schools. As we have pointed out earlier, while some of the schools are very comfortable with being labeled "Islamic," some others are rebranding themselves as schools that offer an "Islamic atmosphere" but are not too different from other private schools.

On the other hand, there are private charter schools that are run by the Gulen network that don't self-identify as "Islamic" in any shape or form; though the network of organizations under the Gulen network are quite traditionally "Muslim" in every sense of the word, both spiritually and in praxis.

We have not included any data from the Gulen schools, and much of our data is drawn from Sunni schools based in immigrant communities, though a few schools based in the African American communities have been included in the data collection.[3] The Gulen network has been the center of controversy since the July 15, 2016 coup attempt in Turkey, for which the Turkish state blames Mr. Fethullah Gulen.[4]

The discourses of global Islam and all its political ramifications – having to do with the current wars in the Middle East – are having an impact on Muslim American institutions. There is seemingly an attempt in the US to tie in these discourses with developments and attempts to suggest that there is massive "radicalization" of Muslims going on across the world.[5]

While at the local level most schools seem to have gained legitimacy as far as their work is concerned, they seem to be impacted by these discourses of global Islam and Islamic radicalization. While these discourses are not new and are steeped in Orientalist imaginations of the "other" East, the legitimacy of these institutions is definitely called into question each time there is a policy shift or an international incident involving the Muslim world.

Islamic Identity

As we have discussed in Chapter 4, Muslim American identity is undergoing a transformation. This means that while Muslim Americans are helping define and solidify a singular identity, this has had other unintended consequences, as we have discussed earlier. The question of identity is one that cannot be settled once and for all, as it is tied to discourses of global migration, economy and Islam in the Middle East and rest of the world and also the movement of ideas and people.

As we have pointed out earlier, while the process of identity making among Muslim Americans has been through "improvisational practices," as GhaneaBassiri points out (GhaneaBassiri, 2012), this can be seen in the realm of Islamic schools as well. While some of the schools surveyed interpret Islamic practices to conform to set practices in the background or tradition of the founders of the school, there is an increasing trend to focus on integrating practices that seek out commonalities with other faith traditions and cultures that are part of mainstream

American society. For example, there is a growing emphasis on understanding other religious traditions or "interfaith" dialogue, even at the school level. This emphasis is new, as some of the interviewees pointed out.

Islam in America is also growing to be an increasingly individualistic religion, as scholars such as Reza Aslan have pointed out. Given that the US is one of the most individualistic countries in the world, where the self comes before the community, there is reason to believe that this trend would apply to Muslim Americans as much as to any other faith-group, he points out.[6] Similarly, Kambiz GhaneaBassiri makes the argument that the supposed incompatibility of Muslim institutions in America is false. He suggests that some have pointed to this "organizational culture and practice" that may not be compatible with the American mainstream (2012, p. 179). The example of Muslim American nonprofits, and schools in particular, demonstrates that this is not true. Consider the nonprofit form of organization, which almost all Muslim American organizations have adopted, that brings together the best of both traditions – a focus on service as well as tax benefits to the donors. While Muslim donors do not primarily give money to charity for tax benefits, we have found in our research that this is definitely an incentive, even if the donors do not consider the tax benefit at first glance.

The binary of Islam and America has existed from the time of Islam's entry into the US and continues to shape discourses of Islam. While GhaneaBassiri points out that this has been an unfortunate trend, it is being challenged both by Muslims and non-Muslims alike. The discourse of interfaith relations is a major deterrent to this narrative. While it seems like the methodological assumptions that many Western scholars have made – about the "East" being primitive and embodying all that is not the "West" – are being challenged, there needs to be a lot more such scholarship for a better understanding of Muslim societies. Western Muslims, as GhaneaBassiri rightly points out, demonstrate the in-betweenness of Islam. The in-betweenness demonstrates, in no uncertain terms, how Islam has been adapted to the local context and has been variously interpreted and reinterpreted by local and immigrant groups.

While there is an attempt to forge the identity of Muslim Americans in a local, all-American fashion, there is no doubt that global discourses of Islam are impinging on this effort.

Public Policy

As we have discussed, public policy towards education and faith-based schools does have an impact on Islamic schools in the US. Whether it is the issue of funding schools through title grants or the question of school vouchers, state funding of Islamic schools remains a key component – and a controversial one – that needs to be addressed. However, at the same time, we found that most of the schools do not want to accept these grants – even while many of them do – as it burdens them with extra regulatory oversight as well as paperwork and so on, which they do not want to undertake. As a school principal in Tennessee pointed out,

> The amount of money we get is definitely not worth the amount of time I have to spend, getting the paperwork moving and making sure we have all the regulatory requirements met. It is too much of a burden for us. I would rather get the equivalent money from the community.

This sentiment was reflected across the board, from various schools that we interviewed.

While those who received funding from the state used it for professional development and related purposes, the board members and the principals are reluctant to let the state mechanism interfere a lot with the education, given that the relationship with the state authorities is a tenuous one, especially at the federal level. While the interactions with state education boards and other bodies are seemingly easy (as reported during our interviews), there seems to be a need among these leaders to not depend on the state as much.

Leadership

The leadership of Muslim American institutions also faces the challenge of helping many of its constituents understand the nonprofit structure. As a board member of a mosque in Tennessee argued, the nonprofit structure is a "necessity" and not a preference. He pointed out that there are several constraints that restrict giving of money to an organization that spends money on administrative necessities like salaries and so on, and he questioned whether zakat and sadaqa money can be spent on those. While he pointed out that there is no need to be "apologetic" about being Muslim, there is definitely a need for Muslims to interact with the existing system, both the educational and the state system, to help frame Islamic practices in a "normal" light.

As a sociological observation this is interesting, because theology is also defined in a social setting by people, and there are many negotiations that theology has to undergo in a society such as the US. His reading of zakat and nonprofits seems to be that of many immigrant groups that are getting used to the nonprofit form for doing social good. Given the significant role of the state, it seemed a bit of an immigrant reading of Islam to us.

Nevertheless, he seemed sincere in his efforts at trying to explain Islamic theology.

The form of leadership that is in play at many of the schools seems to be of an "adaptive" style, where there is a constant need for meaning making and sense making, under conditions of stress. As Ronald Heifetz (2003) has pointed out, this type of leadership is crucial in conditions of extreme stress or even a crisis. Heifetz's analysis suggests that there are situations where leaders have to help make meaning in a culturally defined context that may not be familiar to the followers or to the organization, and thus risk their credibility or legitimacy. This seems to be going on in the case of Muslim American institutions as well.

The climate of fear and suspicion that characterized Muslim communities in the aftermath of 9/11 seems to be returning in the current era, with the Trump administration taking an active position of disengaging with the Muslim communities. The "Muslim ban" on travel from seven Muslim majority countries has also played a big role in alienating the communities; so have plans to refocus the CVE measures only onto the Muslim communities and Islamic radicalism.[7] The CVE measures are, in particular, extremely detrimental to the cohesion of many local communities as they single out Muslim communities for monitoring and surveillance.

If one takes a long-term view of the challenges of leadership development, we will see that there have been three key challenges: (1) building institutions, (2) managing identity and (3) managing crisis. While the first two challenges have been addressed to a satisfactory extent, the final challenge – that of managing a crisis or multiple crises – is something that Muslim communities have yet to address. With several national organizations, such as CAIR and ISNA, putting together training programs and initiatives to help address the growing Islamophobia, there is a feeling that this trend of suspicion of Islam will continue. At the same time as there is fear of the potential for targeting by the US state, there are also efforts being made – most notably by the ISNA – to reach out to the new administration. For instance, the president of ISNA, Imam Magid, participated in the inauguration ceremony's prayer ceremony.[8] His participation in the ceremony has been criticized by other Muslim leaders, who suggest that by participating in it he has undermined the activism of millions of Americans against the divisive politics of Mr. Trump. Imam Magid's defense of his actions is a key reminder, and an often contested one, that there is always a need for Muslim leaders to engage with those in power, even if only to make one's point and to share the teachings of Islam with them. This may well be a pragmatic decision on their part, as it is one based on contingencies.

METHODOLOGY OF TEACHING AND DEVELOPING AN ISLAMIC AND AMERICAN *WELTANSCHAUUNG*

In our interviews, one thing became very clear: the founders of the institutions did not want to impart education that was divorced from values. This meant that issues of faith, community cohesion, loyalty and solidarity were up-front and center for many of the school principals and teachers. While many used the language of faith and Islam to discuss the implications for what kinds of citizens they want to create, there seems to be a sense of imparting a purpose in the lives of these young adults.

The notion of creating "wholeness" among these students is prevalent, as several of our interviewees pointed out. Zahra Al Zeera talks about this in her book *Wholeness and Holiness in Education* (Zeera, 2001).

Almost all interviewees pointed out that the main purpose of incorporating religious studies and other topics such as Moral Science is to help students become "whole" and holistic in their thinking. This means incorporating an epistemology that is deeply Islamic, while aligning it with the best traditions of American secular education.

PRACTICAL IMPLICATIONS

While the debate about public funding for religious schools is likely to pick up in the days to come, it is important to remember that most of the schools that we surveyed sought to stay away from public funding. The reason for this is simple: there were too many strings attached to the public dollars.

In addition, as Lisa Blumerman of the US Census Bureau wrote in 2011, "Of the money received by public school systems, 91 percent came from state and local sources; 9 percent came from the federal government. The $591 billion in total funding in 2009 works out at about $10,499 per pupil, a 2 percent increase from 2008."[9] This means that the share of federal funding is still small, if not negligible. Education is a very local issue, as most scholars of education and public funding of education point out. This means that the zip code of one's residence does play a big role in how one's child is educated. This is all the more reason for gaining a better understanding of how Islamic schools cater to the demands of Islamic education in the US. Given that quality concerns remain paramount among many immigrant communities, there is a legitimate reason for these schools to exist – in addition to the need for culture preservation. These schools provide an alternative venue and a real choice for many parents, who want their children to have a good education.

The Trump administration's appointment of Betsy DeVos as Secretary of Education has raised questions of vouchers and private schools rather strongly. This is the second key area that our work touches upon. As we have argued in this book, most of the schools hesitate to apply for voucher programs, though some do. Many are hesitant –and shared this with us during the interviews – due to bureaucratic hassles, the amount of time it takes them to do the paperwork; while others hesitate due to push back from the governing boards that do not want to seek government funding as it establishes certain preconditions on how exactly the money can be used.

LIMITATIONS OF THIS PROJECT AND FUTURE RESEARCH

We have not sought to delve deeply into the issue of public funding of religious institutions, a debate that has a rich history. We also realize that this issue is a highly controversial one, in which religious groups such as Muslim Americans have been regarded with much suspicion. While scholars such as Underwuffer (2001) have taken the position that public money would be better kept away from religious schools, there are scholars and advocates who have argued for "equal" funding of all religious groups. As Underwuffer points out, since 1940, the Supreme Court has issued more than thirty directives in the field of funding of religious freedom guarantees of the First Amendment in US schools. As she points out, while the principle of separation of state and religion has been accepted, its implementation remains a challenge.

We have not delved into these tensions in much depth, even though we have asked questions pertaining to education vouchers and other forms of support in our survey and interviews.

While our project has looked at the contextual factors that make philanthropy possible, and also the various conditions under which public funding plays out, the debate is far from over. With the incoming Trump administration, issues of public education, funding, role of religious institutions and, in particular, Muslim institutions will be under great scrutiny.

While it is possible to think of Muslim philanthropy and Muslim institution building as part of the great American tradition of philanthropy, often the discourse around it is not framed as such. Our attempt, as scholars of philanthropy, has been to nuance the discussion around Muslim institutions and to show that they are not purely "religious" institutions that are pursuing an ideological agenda, nor are they purely "nonprofits" that are serving people. They blend both the traditions of being "American" institutions in that they embrace both the legal and cultural elements of serving people as well as being rooted in the stories, narratives and myths of what it means to be a "Muslim" in today's America, where many Muslims feel their identity is under threat.

We have attempted to frame the discourse of philanthropy among Muslim American communities in the context of their community development needs and institution building necessities. As we have seen, the demands of legitimacy – both internal and external – have pushed Muslim American communities to embrace and adopt models of community building that are uniquely "American" (Siddiqui, 2014).

NOTES

1. See "How Trump Changed Americans View of Islam – for the Better," available at https://www.brookings.edu/blog/markaz/2017/01/28/how-trump-changed-americans-view-of-islam-for-the-better/?utm_campaign=Brookings+Brief&utm_source=hs_email&utm_medium=email&utm_content=41544610 (accessed February 2017).
2. See "Trump Pushes Dark View of Islam to Center of U.S. Policy-Making," available at https://www.nytimes.com/2017/02/01/us/politics/donald-trump-islam.html?smprod=nytcore-iphone&smid=nytcore-iphone-share&_r=0 (accessed April 2017).
3. For more, see http://gulenschools.org/ (accessed March 2017).
4. For more, see "Turkey Coup: What Is Gulen Movement and What Does It Want?" available at http://www.bbc.com/news/world-europe-36855846 (accessed December 2016).
5. As an example of this rhetoric, see Vice-President Mike Pence's interview in "Trump Travel Ban: States Urge Retention of Temporary Block," available at http://www.bbc.com/news/world-us-canada-38880877 (accessed March 2017). Scholars and activists have pointed out that the "travel ban" on people from the seven Muslim majority countries was also part of the same logic: keeping out Muslims from the US.
6. "Dr. Aslan on the Future of the Middle East," available https://www.youtube.com/watch?v=KzhxSavDkP8 (accessed April 2017).
7. For more, see "Muslim Musicians, Execs Fear the 'Chilling Effect' of Trump's Travel Ban," available at http://www.billboard.com/articles/news/magazine-feature/7677732/trump-immigration-travel-ban-music-industry (accessed March 2017).
8. For more, see "Imam Delivers Message to Trump at Inugural Service," available at http://www.cnn.com/2017/01/20/politics/trump-imam-magid/ (accessed January 2017).
9. See "Funding Public Education," available at https://www.census.gov/newsroom/blogs/random-samplings/2011/05/funding-public-education.html (accessed February 2017).

REFERENCES

Bagby, I. (2011), *The American Mosque: Basic Characteristics of the American Mosque and Attitudes of Mosque*. Washington, DC: Council on American Islamic Relations.

GhaneaBassiri, K. (2012), "Writing Histories of Western Muslims," *Review of Middle East Studies*, 46 (2), 170–179.

Heifetz, R.A. (2003), *Leadership without Easy Answers*. Cambridge, MA: Belknap Press of Harvard University Press.

Siddiqui, S.A. (2014), *Navigating Identity through Philanthropy: A History of the*

Islamic Society of North America (1979–2008). PhD Dissertation, Indiana University.

Underwuffer, L. (2001), "Public Funding for Religious Schools: Difficulties and Dangers in a Pluralistic Society," *Oxford Review of Education*, 27 (4), 577–592.

Zeera, Z. (2001), *Wholeness and Holiness in Education: An Islamic Perspective*. Herndon, VA: The International Institute of Islamic Thought.

Glossary

For ease of use, we have translated some of the commonly used Arabic words. For more exact terminology please refer to http://www.quranicstudies.com.

Black American	Another term for African American
Darura	Necessity
Fatwa	A ruling on a point of Islamic law
Fiqh	Understanding
Iftar	Breaking of the fast during Ramadhan. It also could refer to the meal during Iftar
Ijtihad	Use of reason to arrive at a knowledge of truth in religious matters
Imam	Prayer leader of a mosque
Juma'ah	Friday prayer
Masjid	Mosque
Maslaha	Public welfare
Qur'an	The Holy book of the Muslims. Believed to have been revealed to the Prophet Muhammad
Sadaqa	Voluntary giving of charity
Ummah	The Muslim community or brotherhood. While some scholars have included all the people of the book (Jews, Christians and Muslims), others have translated it to include all living creatures including plants and animals
Zakat	The mandated charity that is to be given by Muslims (roughly translates into 2.5 percent of one's excess wealth). Usually given out during the month of Ramadhan

Index

administrative state 72–74, 80
African Americans
  finding voice for 76
  Gulen schools 129
  indigenous 33
  institutional building 52
  Islamic schools 55–56, 108–109
  move from radical Black
      Nationalism 32
  slavery 51
  studying Muslim Americans within
      context of 4, 6, 62
  tensions between ethnic groups 78
  see also Black American Muslims
American Islam
  "authentic" 43
  crisis in 24–28
  dichotomy 69
  discourse of 36
  "distinct" 73
  growing internationalization of 37
  race/ethnic relations as important
      aspect of 78
  scholars of 62, 76, 79
American laws *ix–xi*
American nonprofit regime
  advantages and limitations *ix*
  unique growth 110
Asad, T. 18–20, 26, 29, 38, 65–66, 71,
    85

Bagby, I. 4, 106, 108, 116, 127
Black American Muslims
  changing discourse of philanthropy
  classification for purpose of study
      20
  first Gulf War of 1990 30–32
  from isolationism to integration
      36–38
  seeking legitimacy from Muslim
      world 43

September 11, 2001 32–35
  social justice 42
  cultural identity as 108
  Malcolm X 17
  see also African Americans
Boin, A. 22–24, 29
Britain *x–xi*

CAIR *see* Council on American–
    Islamic Relations (CAIR)
Catholic schools 55, 60
Catholicism *x–xi*, 65, 70
charity (*zakat*) 23, 39, 41, 54, 70,
    131
Charmaz, K. 110–111, 113
Church of England *x–xi*
Clara Muhammad Schools 56–59,
    107–109, 128
collaboration and conflict 121–122
community philanthropy 60, 122
Coolidge, R.D. 86, 95, 99
Council of Islamic Schools in North
    America (CISNA) 59, 86, 89
Council on American–Islamic
    Relations (CAIR) 7, 27, 48, 53, 63,
    66, 73, 79, 125–126, 132
crisis, definition 22
crisis leadership 23–24
crisis situations
  Great Recession 91, 100–101, 103
  Gulf War, 1990 30–32, 41–42
  philanthropy in 22–24
  September 11, 2001 26–27, 32–35,
      41–42, 91–93, 98–100, 103
"cultural pluralism" 20, 28, 35–36, 40,
    42, 75, 77–78, 128
Curtis, E.E., IV 4, 14, 33–34, 46, 51,
    60, 62, 76, 92, 108

discursive strategic tool, reason as 19,
    38–41